SOCIALIST HISTORY SOCIETY

SOCIALIST HISTORY
OCCASIONAL PAPERS SERIES
NO 12

AN INDIAN LANDSCAPE 1944–1946

JIM FYRTH
2001

ISBN 0 9537742 1 X

Contents

	Reporting a Landscape	3
1	A Passage ...	4
2	... to India	6
3	Sahibs	7
4	Impressions	11
5	A Garden in Bihar	13
6	What is a Country?	16
7	The Unit Parliament and Waterfalls on Sundays	19
8	Mohan and the Raj Bhavan	21
9	Is Your Journey Really Necessary?	23
10	Christmas Tea with a Heroine	26
11	The Jungle and the Paddyfield	29
12	Messengers of the Gods?	32
13	Land, Lots of Land	34
14	Chand Bibi's Fort	35
15	Bombay Spring	37
16	A People Going to Pieces	38
17	Rumblings	39
18	Barefoot Doctors	41
19	Looking for Answers	42
20	One Nation or Two?	44
21	Discordant Voices	46
22	A Visit to the Mahatma	49
23	Echoes of Dickens	53
24	Schooling on Communal Lines?	56
25	Waiting for a Renaissance	58
26	Seeds of Hope	60
27	Kelkhar	62
28	VE Day: Ancient Glories	64
29	VL Night: Present Triumphs	65
30	VJ Day: Preparations for the Future	67
31	Zipper Comes Unzipped	68
32	A Small Paradise	70
33	A Night at the Chinese Opera	71
34	A Storm Drawing Near	73
35	"Where there ain't no Ten Commandments"	76
36	Darker Skies	78

37	To the Mountains	79
38	Home for Christmas!	80
39	Join the Army – See the World	82
40	Politically Unreliable	84
41	Politically Unacceptable	86
42	The Bullshit Boys	89
43	Peace, Murder and a Sudden End	92
44	VIP. A Farewell to Empire	94
	Notes	96

An Indian Landscape 1944–1946

The mighty British
Scattering their power
Beneath the same sky
I know that time will flow along their road too
Float off somewhere the land-encircling web of empire
I know their merchandise-bearing soldiers
Will not make the slightest impression
On planetary paths
Over the ruins of hundreds of empires
The people work

    Rabindranath Tagore, *Recovery 10* (Translated by William Radice)

Reporting a Landscape

How you report a landscape depends on where you were standing when you saw it, and how your view was distorted by the spectacles through which you were accustomed to observe the world. But with a landscape in that foreign country, the Past, there are even greater difficulties. Your memory does not see it as a continuous film, but rather as a collection of old photographs. They have become hopelessly jumbled: in what order should you arrange them? Some are so faded as to defy interpretation; others are perhaps of another landscape and have found their way into the pile by mistake; many are lost altogether. My Indian landscape is recreated with the help, and the difficulties, of such a collection. But it is saved from some of the worst dangers of relying on mental recall alone by notebooks which I kept of certain episodes, helped by old address books. Most importantly, I found, among my sister Paddy's papers after her death, all the letters I had written to her from India. These not only recorded my main activities month by month. They also confronted me with a young man in his late twenties, very sure of himself, opinionated, ready to tell everyone the answers, but fascinated by India, anxious to know more of the country and its people, and keen to make a contribution to what he thought (and still thinks) was the right side in the political and moral conflicts of those stirring and terrible years.

1 A Passage ...

A smell of oil hung heavily over Port Said. It enveloped the quays, where the great ships of the convoy were refuelling, and the decks, where a group of us stood watching the unfamiliar bustle of a Middle Eastern port. It even penetrated into the lower depths of the troop decks, where the less curious sat playing housey-housey. That morning we had, for the first time, seen the sea bright with the coloured sails of the fishing *dhows*, looking from a distance like yachts heeling over before the wind. Now we were looking down at four men in *jellabas* fixing slings to boxes to be hauled up from their small boat and loaded into the hold of the ship. Suddenly a box slipped from its sling and struck one of the men on the chest, knocking him to the bottom of the boat where he lay. After a while, a rope ladder was lowered and a medical officer, in immaculate white uniform, climbed down, stooped over the man without touching him or saying a word, and then climbed up again. The ladder was hauled up. All the afternoon the injured man lay in the bottom of the boat, twitching like a dying snake.

That evening, under the arc lights, the stevedores covered the hatches of the forward well-deck, watched by British soldiers standing along the rails, down the companion ladders, along the sides of the ship. All at once the soldiers started to sing – hundreds of voices raised in one popular song after another. On the hatches the stevedores started to dance, twisting and jumping in a bizarre ballet. The excitement, the bright colours, the background of darkness, the singing and the frantic dancing could, in another language and with other music, have been a moment from a Russian opera.

That night I lay in my hammock thinking about the strange events of the day and our voyage so far.

* * *

When we had embarked at Greenock shortly after D Day, the windows of the tenements had been hung with Union Jacks. People had waved and cheered us, thinking, no doubt, that we were bound for Normandy. But we were going the other way.

At the dockside we had boarded RMS Maloja. Down we had gone to the lowest deck of the ship, where we ate, where at night dozens of hammocks hung, and where silent prayers were said against torpedoes.

As our convoy had gathered and sailed in grey drizzle out of the Clyde, it had met the force of the Atlantic waves. For two or three days we had sailed westward, right into the middle of the Atlantic, making a great loop and heading back towards the Mediterranean. The huge ships had bucked and wallowed, with destroyers fussing around them like sheep dogs looking out for prowling wolves. Once or twice we had seen mines explode.

I had been continually sick, even during life-boat stations, inspections and exercise. Meals were almost impossible. The troop-deck was a misery. But worst of all had been morning toilet. The showers, washbasins and latrines were in the stern of the ship, close to the propeller shaft. The stern rose out of the water, the propellers raced, and then we plunged back again, like some terrifying fairground ride. The smell of hot salt water (we had no other for washing and shaving, and salt-water soap lathers about as well as pumice) mingled with the stink of toilets and the vomit which bespattered the floor was revolting. The only relief from this misery had been to lie down and try to sleep. I started carrying an empty fruit tin so as to avoid the worst ignominies. After four days I was able to walk groggily but, surprisingly, I felt still alive.

In the Mediterranean June these miseries had quickly fallen behind. Breakfast became appetising, after-breakfast exercise a pleasure. Several hundred men and a few women walked quickly round and round the ship, an unbroken chain in each direction, chattering and laughing, passing and re-passing the same people every seven minutes or so. One group which always walked in the opposite direction from ours was of three paratroop Sergeants, the obvious leader with a fine moustache. On his uniform was a single deep red ribbon. I asked him what it was. He told me, "the Order of Lenin". All three had been sent to the Soviet Union to help train paratroops, "but there wasn't much we could teach them; they knew more about it than we did." I suspected modesty, as Orders of Lenin were not given away with a pound of tea, as my mother would have said.

Those who could not stand the atmosphere of the troop-deck, or the everlasting cries of "legs eleven" and "five and nine the Brighton line", now sat around on deck reading and talking. Our group, some of whom had been together since Ballymena, spent hours discussing everything from cabbages to kings, but often arguing politics or the war. We had heard about the V1s, the "buzz bombs", and wondered what the new blitz was like.

Of the group two stand out in memory, Sam Cawthra and the "Shaggy Dog". Sam was a tough, or so he would have people think, humorous and very good company. He would argue anything, even – if he had a credulous listener – that the earth was flat or that mermaids existed. He told us that he had been a Sergeant in the 8th Army in Italy, but had been "busted" down to the rank of signalman because his unit's teleprinters were being sabotaged. One day he had found an Italian civilian interfering with them, had shot him and been court martialled.

Ian Taylor, named Shaggy Dog by a fellow Scot because of his appearance, was a rather jolly instrument mechanic from Edinburgh, a Communist with a tremendous love and considerable knowledge of music and a gargantuan appetite even for troop ship food in an Atlantic gale.[1]

The Mediterranean coasts had slipped past: Gibraltar, which seemed much smaller from the sea than expected, the Spanish Sierra where, eight years earlier, the first battles and atrocities of this war had taken place, Stromboli rising from the sea. Then there were the fishing *dhows*, the smell of oil and the strange ballet at Port Said.

2 ... to India

As the canal wound its way through the desert the ships appeared to be sailing across the sand: then came the terrible heat of the Red Sea, Mount Sinai in the distance, Aden starkly coloured.

Our group began sleeping on deck to avoid the sweat of the troop deck. From that time I slept below on none of my sea voyages, except when it was absolutely necessary. To drift to sleep hearing subdued voices and the sound of the sea against the ship's side, and watching the unfamiliar constellations swinging gently behind the masts was to be filled with joy.

The flying fishes fanned out from under the bows of the Maloja. I understood the Ancient Mariner's complaint about the "bloody sun at noon" – in both senses of the adjective. Each day was very like the last, with some PT and much time for reading and discussion.

We had a few desultory lessons in "Hindustani", the bastard language of the British in India, consisting mostly of verbs in the imperative and nouns for a few necessities and luxuries. An officer gave a talk on India, about there being several hundred languages, the caste system, religious quarrels, the "warrior" peoples, and other scraps of information, mostly to the detriment of the Indians and illustrating the need for the British to be there. I had been reading Palme Dutt's *India Today*, a book criticised by Indian Communists for sectarian attitudes to the nationalist movement, but containing much useful information about the condition of India, and Shelvankar's *Problem of India*, published by Penguin. So I put a different point of view where I was able.

An army MO lectured on personal health care, how we should avoid "heat exhaustion", formerly called "sun-stroke", and should not over-expose our bodies. Heavy sunburn was punishable as a self-inflicted wound if precautions had not been taken. He told us about some of the pleasures awaiting us, such as prickly heat and malaria. He explained how the female anopheles mosquito, who carries malaria, would be after our blood to fertilise her eggs, so that we should have to take daily Mepacrime tablets (which turned some people yellow) and that it was an offence not to cover our arms and legs at night. He ended by warning about VD, against which he recommended abstinence, adding, "if you must do it, find a goat", which about summed up the British lack of reality on the subject. The army did not issue condoms, nor were they easily available.

The American army did issue them. Its canteens displayed posters such as one of a "pin-up" with the admonition, "Don't risk it fella! Wear a sheath". One day shouts of laughter rose from all the ships. Bobbing over the waves, with a following breeze which kept them up with the convoy, were dozens of condoms which GIs had inflated and thrown overboard. All the ships were leaning towards the centre of the convoy as laughing men and women crowded the rails. Then the order came, "stand by – life-boat stations", and the ships sailed on on even keels.

These Americans had joined the convoy at Port Said, some were on the Maloja. One GI from South Carolina commented that British soldiers treated Egyptians badly. Ian Taylor asked, "Aren't black people treated badly in the southern states?" to which he replied, "The nigger ain't treated badly. But he knows his place."

Near the Indian coast we met the monsoon, and when we entered Bombay harbour the shore looked very much like the Firth of Clyde had when we set out.

3 Sahibs

Heavy rain fell ceaselessly over Bombay during that day in July when we landed and were taken in our monsoon capes to the Bombay Central railway station, where we first saw the squalid hovels of corrugated iron and matting around the railway and in the outskirts of the city. They were a sight for which even those of us who had read about Indian poverty were not prepared.

Then came the first villages; earthen houses with tiled roofs through which smoke filtered into the rain, small earthen walled compounds for the animals and lanes of mud. Occasionally a man with a sack wrapped round him, or a woman with her wet sari clinging to her, walked by a roadside. Sometimes a white-clad figure carrying an umbrella slopped with bare feet through the puddles. We heard, for the first time, the croaking of thousands upon thousands of frogs, welcoming the monsoon as their mating time, their voices drowning the sound of the rain, and even the rattle of the train.

In the morning we reached Mhow, a place which was to India what Catterick was to Britain – the Signals Training Centre. Here we were to have a refresher course and acclimatise to India, in more senses than one. Indore, in which Mhow was the main British presence, was a "native state", ruled autocratically by the Maharaja of Holkar with a British "Political Officer" to advise him, so that he would do nothing to upset the Raj. Cutting off the hands of petty thieves, still then the practice in Indore, did not rank as endangering British rule.

The barrack rooms were tall, one storey, airy, stone buildings, with a stone verandah running the length of one side, behind Norman style arches. Along two sides were our *charpoys* – the wooden framed beds with sisal networks in place of springs, which were the universal Indian resting place. Each had a grey, wooden kit-box and a mosquito net. On the high ceilings were large fans (*punkahs*) which provided a draught for the room.

Across the road from the barrack a long building housed the latrines. Each cubicle had a wooden seat over a bucket, which at night was taken out through a trap at the back by untouchables, men on the lowest rung of Hindu society. It was part of old soldiers' mythology that, on the North West Frontier, the tribesmen were liable to open the trap and, with a sharp sword, deprive the seated man of his all.

After the voyage it was a descent to Earth to be stationed in a depot, with its "stand by your beds" for kit inspections – everything laid out according to a pattern, boots with soles upwards and studs polished. Reveille was at 5.30 a.m., followed by PT and arms drill, the curious 18th century ritual still then practised by the British army. For the first week there was also "square bashing" – just to make sure we had not forgotten. Breakfast was from 7.30-8.30, then classrooms until dinner time, and from 2.30 bed until 4 p.m. This was a welcome time for sleeping, reading and writing letters. Then there was another hour's classroom, after which we were at leisure.

The food slapped on to our plates as we queued in front of the barrack was abominable. The "beef" must have come from aged water buffaloes; no amount of cooking could have made it palatable. Worse were "soyalinks", sausages made of soya, at which even the starving dogs which hung around the barracks turned up their noses. Often I preferred to buy bananas and a pot of cream from the "fruit-wallah" on the verandah. If edible, the food had to be guarded from swarms of flies and from the kites, known to the soldiers as "shite-hawks". These birds sat along the roof, dived over the unwary soldier and, with a bang on the enamel plate, carried off the whole meal. Twice I was a victim.

But there were compensations. On Sunday we did no manner of work. Also, we had sheets, for the first time in the army, a "gift from the people of India". Since most Indians themselves did not own sheets, this was generous! Nor were we able to thank them in person as we were ordered not to speak to them.

This injunction came in the course of two lectures, given on our arrival by the OC Signals Training. He warned us about the NW Frontier. The frontiersmen, he said, were given to raiding and fighting, so the Government paid them subsidies to keep quiet. When a new regiment came out the payments were stopped. The tribes resumed their usual practices and the new troops were given battle experience. Bang went another imperial legend; boys' stories, Henry Newbold poems and stirring cinema epics.

More sinister was his denigration of the Indians who were, it appeared, not much good at anything. No wonder the farmers were poor, we had only to look at the ridiculously large ricks they built. No English farmer would dream of building them so large. He seemed not to have realised that there were climatic/thermal reasons for the different practices. Then he said, "Now! I've seen some of you chaps talking to the Indians around the place, calling them 'Jack' or 'Johnnie'. Now I don't want to see any of you talking to Indians. You must remember that you are here as an army of occupation and that any one of you is better than anyone in this country."

I discovered what he meant. The *charwallah* on the verandah had a small boy helping him, to whom I chatted. The father (I can still visualise their faces and the boy's thin limbs) asked if I had a spare pair of socks, as his son had always wanted socks; he had no shoes. I gave him a pair of army woollens. In return the father started to teach me a few words of Hindi. At one lesson a passing Sergeant called me aside. "If", he said, "I see you talking to that man again I will put you on a court-martial charge. When you are at home you can be a Communist, or anything you like, but here you could be responsible for women and children being murdered in their beds." After that I exchanged a friendly word with the *charwallah* only when purchasing his wares. I did not want him to lose his livelihood, or to be put on a charge myself. His little boy wore the socks until they were stiff with dirt and his feet came through the soles.

Looking back, I can see not only the arrogance of an imperial people, but also the fear felt by those who had served the Raj during the previous years. No longer self-confident, as before the war, they had felt in 1942 that they might be living in the last days. The British army had been defeated and driven out of South East Asia; the Japanese were on Indian soil. Congress had demanded that Britain quit India, tens of thousands of suspects had been arrested. There had been riots and bombs. Then came the year of famine in Bengal. How many died? Two million? Four million? Over wide areas village society collapsed. Now, although the Japanese had been driven from India and the country was quiet, there was tension. Those who came out with high-minded sympathy for Indian aspirations must have seemed potential traitors.

I discovered too, that as Kipling had recorded, the regular soldiers who spent years in India were also victims. In 1944 there were many who had been due to go home when the war started, but who were still detained there. Many of them hated the country and hated the people. One such was a Corporal who was being retrained with us. One day he told how us he had knocked down an old woman while driving his "garri" (truck). "I didn't want her reporting me," he said, "so I backed the truck over her to finish her off." When the rest of us expressed horror he shrugged, "When you've been here as long as I have you get to hate these people." Another time he told us how, when he was serving in Bengal during the famine, an Indian clerk in the regimental office had invited him to his home. There he said that he and his wife were starving. They had agreed that if he gave them 30 rupees, (less than £2, about £40 in today's money) the husband would go out, leaving the wife alone with the corporal. Someone asked what happened. "I beat him down to 20 rupees," he boasted, "and after that, whenever I wanted to I took a bag of rice and the husband went out."

Most British soldiers easily saw themselves as superior to people whom they never met socially as equals, whose ways they did not understand and whose food they hated. Men who had been obliged to call others "sir" all their lives were now themselves addressed as "sahib", and had their washing and tailoring done for them for very small sums of money. When I saw them laughing as they poured water over a skinny child who was begging by the railway line, or drunkenly abusing civilians and forcing them off the pavement, I realised how both the Indians and British were damaged by the OC's doctrine.

4 Impressions

Three miles from Mhow was our swimming pool among pleasant trees, with the peaks of the Vindya Hills rising, green and tempting behind it. Once, with a companion I climbed to the tops of the hills, but the grass was long and tough and walking was not pleasant.

To the bazaar we went by *tonga*, a two-wheeled vehicle, with bells and decorations jangling from the horse and two or three passengers sitting under a fringed awning, backs to the horse. In the bazaar was a cinema that showed American films. Sometimes the reel broke, or reels were put on in the wrong order. Then there would be shouts and calls, usually of a racist nature, from the troops.

To enter the bazaar or town was to be transported to medieval Europe. The streets were narrow. Alleyways with murky liquid running down them branched off. Shopkeepers sat outside their premises calling on passers-by to purchase. There were mangy "pyard" dogs, horrible smells, and everywhere beggars – old women with shrivelled breasts, young women with babies on their hips, the cripples and the blind. But there was movement and bright colours, and always the cheerful, jangling sound of popular Indian music.

My first impressions of Indians were of their gentleness and dignity, though later I had experience of the opposites. But the gentleness when they spoke and that of the white-clad young men holding hands in the street, and the dignity of the women, especially of the little girls walking to school, with their black pigtails and their schoolbooks balanced on their heads, were lovely to see.

In the bazaar was a bookshop. In India there were bookshops even on provincial railway stations. I began adding to the small collection I had brought with me. To hold them I bought a tin trunk with my name and number painted on it.

In barracks there were gramophone recitals three times a fortnight. There would be a Beethoven night, a Mozart night with the "Jupiter" and arias from the operas, and sometimes a twentieth century night. In those days there were only "seventy-eights", and the sound quality would be unacceptable today, but it was a pleasure to listen to the "Pastoral Symphony" with the monsoon outside. Because these recitals were encouraged in the army thousands of men and women, who had had few opportunities and perhaps little desire to listen to music, learned, in out of way places, to love it.

The other delight offered by Mhow was the "Thrift Shop", run on payday by the memsahibs, the wives of regular officers at the depot. As soon as we had received our pay we would dash along to be ahead of the queue, so that, for a small amount, we could purchase a good tea or snack. We could also buy stationery and toiletries at less than bazaar prices. And, once a week, we could sit in comfortable chairs and read English magazines. Naturally there was no social contact between the mems and the BORs, but we were glad of their once-a-week service.

It was on the walks to and from the swimming pool that I first saw village India at close quarters. We passed bullock carts with their unsteady wheels, their bells tinkling and their hurricane lamps hanging beneath their axles. We met farmers walking with sticks in their hands, followed by their wives, carrying bundles on their heads and infants on their hips. We saw women drawing water from the wells and moulding cow dung into cakes, to be dried on the walls of their houses for fuel. On the hillsides small boys and girls tended goats and sheep. Their shrill, plaintive pipes carried a great sense of peace. When they saw us they rushed down with the constant cry, "Baksheesh, Sahib, Sahib, Baksheesh!"

The fields were green after rain, and where there was a clump of trees in the distance, it was almost possible to imagine that it was English countryside. That was, until you saw the poverty of the villages and encountered the smell – a mixture of rancid ghee, burning cow dung and human ordure. It was unbearable to unaccustomed noses, even at half-a-mile.

The first shock of India made me feel that one's heart would break unless it became hardened to the sights and smells of poverty and human wastage. Unless it were possible to believe that the Indian people could make a better future, there was a danger of ending up hating the country and its people. Many did.

After we had been in Mhow a few weeks, there was an invitation to volunteer to work with the British mission in China. Those chosen would be instructed in Calcutta and flown "over the Hump" (the Himalayas) to Chungking, then the seat of the Chinese government. I volunteered, but was not chosen. Instead I was to go to Ranchi, in Bihar in the East of British India.

When I left, the *charwallah* brought a garland of paper flowers and put it round my neck, but I was too embarrassed to wear it. Then he asked me for the annas that he had paid for it. His little boy was still wearing the shreds of my cast-off socks.

5 A Garden in Bihar

At Khandwa Junction the mail train which was to take us on the second leg of our journey to Ranchi was eighteen hours late. Monsoon floods had breached the embankment. So the three of us, two older NCOs and myself, had to sit it out. The waiting room benches provided beds, the refreshment room fried eggs, chips and sweet tea. Indian eggs being little bigger than bantam eggs, it took four to make a meal: on that journey we each ate sixteen fried eggs, the binding effect of which was welcome once we had taken a glance at the "facilities" provided by the junction. The station also had a bookstall, with newspapers, and it was here that I had my first experience of the wilder fringes of the nationalist press.

When we changed from the mail train to the line for Ranchi, we were ordered on no account to leave the train until it reached our destination. Bihar had not suffered from the famine of the previous year as Bengal had done, but epidemics – cholera, typhoid, smallpox and plague – were sweeping through eastern India. Each day the *Calcutta Statesman* reported the number of dead bodies collected from the Calcutta streets. There were rarely less than a hundred and often more than two hundred. Beside the railway, crowds of men, women and children, many sick, some dying, called for *baksheesh*. We were not even permitted to open the windows.

At Ranchi we were taken outside the city where my companions of the last two days disappeared into a large camp on one side of the road while I went through iron gates and up a gravel drive to a large bungalow on the other. Here the surprises began. No 3 Company HQ Signals India turned out to be a small training centre for women, in their late teens and early twenties, of the Women's Auxiliary Corps (India), the Indian counterpart of the ATS. There were a few Indian and Anglo-Indian women and a larger contingent from Nepal. These had volunteered for the war because their fathers, brothers and boy-friends were Gurkha soldiers in the Indian Army and they wanted to be soldiers too. Unlike the Indians, they were noisy and full of fun. When they arrived, and for occasions, they wore beautiful saris. They were learning to operate telephones, radios and switchboards. The cultural leap must have been staggering. Many came from villages where the most advanced technology was the wheel, and there were not many of those. To reach these villages when they went home, they had to ride on horseback for two days after leaving the train.

To instruct them and feed and administer the unit were some dozen British NCOs. I was immediately raised to the rank of Lance Corporal –

paid! (Most L/Cpls were "acting unpaid"). We ate in the bungalow but slept and lived in tents in the large garden, the most striking feature of which was a *shaduf*, by which water was raised from the well exactly as it had been in Egypt of the Pharaohs. Between the top of two posts was fixed a long pole with about four feet towards the well and twenty feet on the other side. When this long lever was pulled down a bucket of water was raised from the well.

The other surprise was an Indian CO, a reserved, military-looking man, holding a King's Commission as Major. There was no apparent resentment among the British troops at taking orders from an Indian – not that he gave many. Besides an English Captain there were two Sikh officers, a *Jemidar* and a *Subadar*, with Viceroy's Commissions equivalent to Major and Captain. They had authority over the women and the Indians who catered for them, but not over the British staff. The senior of the two was a large, ebullient man, whose pet goat followed him, bleating, everywhere, like Mary's lamb. It lived in his tent, which occasioned ribald comments from the British. Our two cooks were both "regulars". One was a plump, rather coarse, but jolly Irishman (inevitably "Paddy"). The other was a tall, red skinned, raw-boned man, who lived in the same tent as I did, would discuss any topic seriously and recited Kipling's longer "soldier" poems – *The Ladies*, *Gunga Din*, and others, from memory.

My job was to repair the instruments – radios and telephones – used in the training, and also, when necessary, repair fuses, connect plugs, change bulbs and wire lamps, in the bungalow. To perform these not onerous duties I had a workshop, reached by steps to a platform which looked over the hedge towards a village half-a-mile away.

We were all warned that "hanky-panky" with the women was absolutely forbidden, that the "Nepalese would be willing – but no!" Certainly I saw no signs of such. There was, on the contrary, real affection from the students towards their instructors, and when one had to leave there were many tears and cries of, "Our Sir is leaving us." But one night, when a group of us returned from the cinema, we learned that the garden had been invaded by Gurkha troops, carrying their *kukris* (lethal looking curved short swords). Rumour had reached them that we were training their women for the army brothels, and they were going to put a stop to it. Only with great difficulty, and by the women themselves, had they been persuaded otherwise and had withdrawn their forces.

The two cooks were, in Kipling's words "taking their fun where they found it". Paddy was picking up Anglo-Indian girls at dances in the city. My tent mate had his "steady", a young married woman in the village. From my workshop I could see him sloping off across the fields when the mid-day meal had been cleared away. She was at that time working in the garden, one of a group maintaining the gravel paths, and he introduced her to me – she smiled shyly when he spoke – telling me with pride that he had had her small son vaccinated, and showing me the pad and bandage on his little arm.

Ranchi, though a substantial city, was little westernised. Cows wandered right in the broad main street, and almost naked *sadhus*, with their staffs and begging-bowls were given annas by well-fed shopkeepers sitting outside their stores, so assuring grace for both the giver and receiver. Always there were beggars – the infirm aged, women with babies, and those whose limbs had been broken and distorted in infancy by syndicates which had bought them from hungry parents. These human wrecks now appealed to passers-by with sad uncomprehending eyes, to fill the syndicates' coffers. The city also had a cinema and a Chinese restaurant. On my first visit of exploration I entered this restaurant and, as it was crowded, had to share a table with a military policeman. He had nearly finished and, as he got up to leave, I asked if he had paid. His answer was a step in my education: "If they made us pay we would put the place out of bounds to troops."

But at dusk India took on its other mood of awe-inspiring beauty. Then the odorous alleyways, the beggars, the mad dog that went screaming up the road after being shot by a military policeman, were hidden, and the overwhelming scent was that of the lovely queen of the night tree. Only the temple on the hill stood outlined against the evening. The sky, from East to West and from North to South, became flecked with all shades of red and oyster blue. The "flying foxes", the great fruit bats with their two-foot wing span, left the banyan trees and flapped overhead in flocks, to spend the night robbing the orchards of the farmers.

Now, in October, the rains had abated and Ranchi, at two thousand feet above the plains, passed each day through the cycle of the English year. The mornings were like a fresh spring day at home; by early afternoon the heat was that of a good English summer; the evenings were autumn and the nights a crisp English winter. With nightfall, plaintive singing and the complicated rhythms of drums started up from all the villages around, celebrating the end of a successful monsoon. From the road I watched some twenty young men and women beside a large corn stack, circling and swaying in the moonlight to the accompaniment of the drums and singing as they danced, each with their hands on the hips of the one in front – boy, girl, boy, girl. At the end of October came Diwali, the Hindu festival of lights which marks the beginning of winter. In the windows and at the doors of the houses the little flickering lights made the night enchanting.

At this season the wild creatures were active and I could watch them from my workshop. One morning I returned to a radio that I was working on to find that the blue-print had been torn into small pieces to make, among the valves and wires, a nest for six little pink, blind mice. It hurt to think that perhaps the mother mouse was watching when I killed them and they were devoured by ants. The large black ants were everywhere, while the tent-ropes, bed-legs and kitbags were in danger of disintegrating beneath the layers of earth-paste made by white ants. Paddy the cook dug up a nest of white ants and, within seconds, an army of black ants marched out of a hole in the ground, seized the wriggling termites and bore them down to their underworld. At night, on the walls of the rooms in the bungalow, lizards scuttled after insects. Once, when I was on guard (which meant sitting in the office reading) a lizard seized a praying mantis and a great battle took place, the still fighting mantis disappearing slowly into the lizard.

6 What is a Country?

Shortly after I joined the Company, the CO told me to take charge of the rest and information room. The job was to keep up-to-date a large map of Europe on the wall, moving pins and silk to indicate the changes in the fronts, East, West, and South. From the radio news and the press I chose items to make into a "wall newspaper". I had also to ensure that there were pamphlets and newspapers available. The rest room was the one place where there were comfortable chairs.

One day I found myself on a charge before the CO for "neglect of duty while on active service". It sounded terrible. As I stood to attention the Major told me that I had neglected to record the most recent advances of the Red Army on the map! For this I was admonished.

He also said that he wanted the women to be told what the war was about and what we were fighting for. There were language difficulties, but the WAC(I) Lance Corporal was a Nepalese who taught in a mission school in Khatmandu and spoke English fluently. I was already teaching her how various instruments worked so that she could help her countrywomen to master them. The next few sessions together were in the rest room with a map of Europe on the table. She was very stylish in her uniform, silk stockings and Max Factor makeup, but her picture of the world belonged to the days of the Holy Roman Empire. All Europe, she thought, owed allegiance to the King Emperor. Our allies, De Gaulle and Tito, she believed were Englishmen. Hitler, it seemed, was leading a revolt (rather like Gandhi) and must be put down. The Germans, she had been told, did not believe in God.

I explained from the map, that Germany, France, all those different colours, were separate countries. "What", she asked, "do you mean by a country?" "What is a nation?" Good questions: how do you answer them? Concerning Hitler there were further difficulties. I told her that he had been a Lance Corporal in the First World War. "That", she said, "is impossible". A Lance Corporal could not become a ruler. We tried our best together, but what the women were told I cannot think. At that time you couldn't tell anyone in India that we were fighting for democracy! She simply would not have understood the word.

The CO then asked me to give two talks, one to the Indians and one to the Nepalese, about women in the Soviet Union and their part in the war effort. I was to use short words, and the Lance Corporal would translate if necessary. I spoke, as we did in those days, of how Soviet women were paid the same as men and did men's work in war factories, even as managers and engineers, and of the role of women in the armed forces. I do not recall the Indian reaction, but the Gurkha women were enthusiastic and all wanted to be snipers or partisans.

At Ranchi I first made contact with the Communist Party of India (CPI). I recall meeting the secretary, in the city, where he called a rickshaw and we rode out to Karam Kothi, Mr D K Chaudhuri's bungalow. It was the only time I travelled by rickshaw and I felt very uncomfortable being pulled by a human horse. Where *tongas* were not available we took "tricshaws" propelled by pedal power. Embarrassment increased when the rickshaw man argued fiercely with the secretary over the fare, pointing at me as justifying his demand for extra.

Chaudhuri was a lawyer with an ascetic Bengali face. The three of us had not been talking for long when there was a shuffling outside the window and a face looking in. The secretary ran out, but the intruder was disappearing. Chaudhuri was convinced that it was not a thief.

They told me about the work of the CPI in Bihar, mainly among the peasants, many of whom they organised into the *Kissan Sabha* (roughly Peasant League or Assembly). I learned also of the devastation of the famine in Bengal, and how much of its rural society had collapsed. Villages had disintegrated, and hundreds of thousands had migrated towards the towns. Some quarter of a million women had taken to prostitution to live, thousands of women had gone to work, for a few annas a day, under crooked contractors, building the roads along which the armies had pushed into Burma and the Arakan. As the secretary was a working class man with very little English much of this had to be translated by Chaudhuri. Karam Kothi was quite near our unit, so I went straight there on a subsequent visit.

My colleagues in the unit were not very political, though they were not Tories and their attitudes were anti-Establishment. There was absolutely no anti-communism or hostility towards my views, only a certain scepticism. When, in mid-October, I was adopted as Communist candidate for Wembley in the forthcoming election, they were pleased that of "one of us" was standing. There was a great deal of leg-pulling. I was addressed as "the Honourable and Gallant Member for Wembley" and told that, of course, if elected I would go over to the other side and support James Grigg, the very unpopular Minister for War. At that time it was thought that the Wembley constituency would be divided into three, and the CP thought there was a chance of winning the seat based on the factory area and council estates of Alperton. In the event, there were only two constituencies. I was withdrawn. Both seats were won by Labour in 1945, and when I wrote to congratulate the new MP for Wembley South he thanked me for the support which I and the Party had given him.

Though pleased to have been selected, I was concerned about the effect the news would have on Mother and Father. So I wrote at once, explaining and saying that, in the circumstances of the time, it was quite normal, and stressing that it would mean my earlier return home and discharge from the army. Unfortunately, before my letter could reach home, the *Daily Express* picked up the story ("L/Cpl serving in Far East etc."), and I was worried that that would be the way they heard about it.

But before anything could be said there was a shock. One Sunday afternoon in early November I was reading in my tent, when the office clerk brought me a cablegram to say that Mother had died suddenly on 25 October. Nothing else. The cable had been routed through Delhi, where someone had delayed in finding me. Anger at the delay, combined with the shock of the news, meant some bleak days, lightened by letters from family and friends and the sympathy of my colleagues.

Three weeks later the CO said that, although he was very sorry, orders had come for me to leave the unit. The 14th Army was pushing the

Japanese back in Burma, and all able-bodied men were needed. I must join an operational unit. No more lotus eating in a Bihar garden. I was to return to Mhow and await posting.

7 The Unit Parliament and Waterfalls on Sundays

At Mhow, a "unit parliament", with seventy to a hundred "members" had grown out of a discussion group. Official blessing had been given to a "government" and a "left-wing opposition"; but to keep it going left-wingers had made up most of both, so the "government" had resigned. The "house" then split into a "centre party", a "right-wing party" and a large "left-wing party". This had formed a new "government", which had introduced a number of progressive measures for debate and vote. Suddenly, after one very lively session, the whole venture was suspended by orders from above. This was six months after the more famous Cairo Parliament had been suppressed.

There had also been a "parliament" at Deolali, the large depot and transit camp in Bombay Province, during 1944. There were probably others, and other suppressions, which have not been recorded, where education officers sought to prepare the troops for the coming elections and traditional military men took fright at political discussion in the ranks.

The "parliament" at Mhow had brought together a number of left-wing BORs, who could exert a greater influence in the depot, and contact the like-minded arriving from Britain or, like myself, passing through. Life at Mhow had become more interesting.

One evening three of us walked to a nearby village and stood in the street talking to the swarm of children who rushed upon us for the sweets we had brought. They talked to us in English because, as they explained, their village had a free school, financed by the Maharajah of Holkhar, and where, every day, they were given free milk. In Bihar there had been one school – not free and no milk – for every ten or fifteen villages. The difference was evident. These children knew something of what was happening in the world beyond their own fields. Then they showed us their well, which had a pump to draw the water; the pump was also the property of the Maharajah. Although their homes were crumbling back into the earth and the dusty street would be a quagmire in the monsoon, the children were proud of the school and the pump.

At Mhow as "billet orderly" I had to sweep the barrack room floor after breakfast, a job which took half an hour. Just before the mid-day meal the post had to be collected and distributed, which took another half hour. The rest of the "working day" I read, wrote letters and guarded against thieves. It was restful but not of much help to the war-effort.

I had many letters from friends and family. Bill Carritt,[2] who was with the artillery pushing towards Mandalay, wrote occasionally. Harry Welford[3] kept me in touch with politics at home and sent the *Daily Worker*, *Labour Monthly*, and books and pamphlets which did the rounds.

Harry also sent me *British Soldier in India*, a selection from Clive Branson's letters to his wife Noreen. Clive had fought in the International Brigade in Spain, had been taken prisoner and condemned to death but released in an exchange of prisoners. Earlier in 1944 he had been killed in the Arakan. He was an artist and a poet, and his descriptions of India, its scenery, its people and politics were so real and true to me. My copy is dog-eared from the many hands through which it passed during the next two years. These letters were an antidote to a poisonous book by the gossip writer Beverley Nichols, who had visited India for a few weeks – some spent in hospital – and produced his *Verdict on India*, which sentenced the accused to the gallows. Hinduism, with its erotic sculptures and a few remaining temple prostitutes, was "the religion of the red lamp", Congress was a fascist organisation, caste was all pervasive, even in the Roman Catholic Church (whose rituals in the mass he got wrong), Indian music and art were minor achievements. His book gave respectability to the prejudices of those who would say of Indian soldiers: "We shake the trees and those with tails we throw back, the others we put into uniform." So Branson was a good ally.

On Sundays the billet managed without an orderly. Four of us from the "left-wing party" would walk to Patelpani, a lovely onomatopoeic name for a scene dominated by a series of waterfalls (*pani*=water). After four miles along a rocky path into the Vindya Hills, there was the main waterfall, dropping a hundred feet into a gorge, whose steep sides were covered with scrubby jungle. Down the rough path through the bushes I shuffled on my bottom, taking care not to look down. Of three pools the first, churned by the falling water, was unsafe for swimming. The third was believed locally to house an evil spirit; the sceptical said a crocodile. Whichever it was, no one swam there; the steep rocky sides would have made it difficult to get out. Depot mythology had it that a reckless soldier who had dived in never resurfaced, and was never found. I can believe that he was stunned by the freezing water.

The second pool was so cold that all we could do was to swim across and climb on to the rocks to thaw out in the sun before crossing again. Then the *charwallah* who, goodness knows how, had brought his large tea urn and cakes down the steep ravine was as welcome as manna in the desert. No one argued with his monopoly prices. We never saw the crocodile nor felt, in that place of peace and beauty, any influence of the evil spirit. Neither did we see the panther, though climbing through the scrub we were assaulted by a smell like a thousand tom cats. Perhaps he was watching us – or sleeping. It would have been good to see him – at a distance. We did see a cobra which hurried across our path, and the baboons who sat on the rocks, conferring like the War Cabinet. By the end of the walk back to barracks we could just about limp into the music evening.

Christmas cards were arriving from home when orders came for me to proceed (no one in the army ever went anywhere, they "proceeded") to Poona to join the Headquarters Signals of the 50th Indian Tank Brigade, there preparing to go into Burma.

8 Mohan and the Raj Bhavan

The interesting way from Mhow to Poona was through Bombay, but my instructions were to go across country. So I went through Bombay.

Bill Carritt had suggested that I call and see his friend Mohan at the Raj Bhavan. From Victoria Terminus (we called it VT; it is now Subhas Bose[4] Terminus), the baroque monument to the Raj and its railway engineers, where the old queen sat in marble state in the forecourt, I took a taxi to Sandhurst Road. This was a broad street of offices and apartments not far from the Marine Drive (now Subhas Bose Drive). The Raj Bhavan included the head office of the Communist Party of India (CPI), the editorial office of *People's War* (the party's newspaper), a bookshop, a library and the commune of the party officers and their families.

Mohan Kumaramangalam was a member of the party's central committee, and used to see British communists and other left wingers who were passing through Bombay, tell them about the political situation in India and give them addresses of people they might like to see wherever they were going. It was an informal but effective form of organisation.

Mohan, his sister Parviti and brother Kuma had been students in England in the 1930s, Mohan at Cambridge, Parviti at Oxford. I had met her in 1940 in London, when Mohan and her parents had been interned in India under the "emergency". Now she lived in Bombay with her husband Krishnan. Their parents were well-off leaders of the Congress Party in Southern India, and were called, for reasons I do not understand, Suberan. Their mother had been one of India's representatives, together with

Gandhi, at the Round Table Conference in London in 1931, called to discuss a constitution for India.

Mohan and Parviti were both handsome and charming and devoted to Indian independence and to socialism. Once, Mohan told me, laughing, that but for Marx he might have become a Proustian. The Nehrus were family friends of the Suberans, and when Indira Gandhi became Prime Minister she made Mohan Minister of Transport. He was killed when his plane crashed in a dust storm. Parviti and Krishnan both became Communist Members of the *Lok Sabha* (Parliament). Kuma became a top executive in Indian Airlines. An older brother, Para, who was a Brigadier in the Indian Army, became the Commander-in-Chief after independence. Mohan and I became friends and spent time together whenever I was in Bombay. I have pleasant memories of us walking together near the sea, late in the evening when there was nearly always a cool breeze off the water.

Once, passing through Bombay, I was unwell and was put to bed at the Raj Bhavan, in a cool, darkened room, where I was nursed by a young woman who was a trained nurse, in a calm silence. Her two year old son stared at me with his large brown eyes and hid his face in his mother's sari when I spoke to him.

Many times I took my mid-morning meal in the commune. After washing hands and feet under a tap in the yard we sat cross legged round the cloth spread on the floor. I loved the soured milk, dahl, chapattis and curried vegetables which were the staple diet. Once I ran into a Wembley acquaintance who had been a shop stewards convenor at one of the factories.

"Do you know", he said, "they eat with their fingers? Some of them have been to Oxford and Cambridge, but they eat with their fingers. Someone ought to speak to them about it."

I had learned that particular skill, and Mohan explained that northern Indians, who did not dirty their fingers beyond the first joint, looked down on southern Indians because they dirtied theirs to the second joint.

People came and went as they moved about the sub-continent, but some were always there. I remember the Charis and their ten year old son, Lialit, who became a great friend, always glad to see me. We promised to write to each other when I returned home. I think we did – once. The matriarch of the commune was "our Mai", the manager, housekeeper and provider of meals, the "Earth Mother" of the Party, a dignified, stout, grey-haired woman, who said little but was much loved and respected. When I called towards the end of my time in India, Lialit came running towards me in tears, crying "Our Mai is dead". Her funeral had been the previous day. I think she was his grandmother.

Among those passing through, I recall a large, ebullient Moslem in white jodphurs and a Gandhi cap, who had been arrested in Afghanistan and displayed in a public cage in the streets of Kabul. There was "Doc" Adhikari, the Party Chairman, urbane and always ready with a laugh when we met. We re-met in 1947 when he came to the conference of Commonwealth Communist Parties in London. S A Dange, Secretary of the All-India TUC appeared from time to time. He was a veteran of the Meerut Conspiracy trial of 1929-33,[5] when the Indian Government, attempting to crush the growing trade union movement, had arrested 32 leading trade unionists, including four Britons, and meted out savage sentences after a three-and-a-half year trial. His silent solemnity seemed a result of that time.

I met others who were veterans of those underground days, S V Ghate, another of the Meerut prisoners, Ranadive and Mirajkhar. Ghate told me how the trial was held in a village, far away from anywhere there might be support for trade unions. The five "assessors" – there was no jury – were peasants, village headmen, who could not understand the issues and were often asleep. When the trial ended one of them said, "These are good men, but whether they are guilty is hard to say." But Justice Yorke, who presided, would have none of it; "These men claim to represent the people – put them in the lowest class of prisoner." Fortunately the gaol superintendent, Rutherford, who liked to mix with the prisoners, phoned Delhi and got the order rescinded. Even so, Dange had to wear an iron collar at first. Their prison conditions improved, but they went on hunger-strike because they were isolated from the other prisoners. Sanitary conditions were good by day but bad by night. There was no protection from mosquitoes. The diet was rice and dhal, but food and milk could be bought with a bribe. All the prison staff took bribes; even the appalling medical care could be improved with a bribe. When five of the prisoners escaped the superintendent said, "I can't trust you", and exercise was stopped. The Communist prisoners formed a "cell", which impressed the other prisoners, and they won over all of the Congress Socialist Party leaders who were in the gaol.[6]

9 Is Your Journey Really Necessary?[7]

Passengers on the Madras mail train, as it climbs the escarpment of the Western Ghats on its way towards Poona, can enjoy the most spectacular scenery in Western India. On one side the mountains rise steeply, covered with tropical jungle trees, on the other they fall precipitously to the coastal plain. I was to make the journey, up or down, many times; with monsoon clouds pouring over the peaks and through the passes, and with the summer sun wilting the forest trees; but the first sight was the most exciting.

The line is a tribute to British railway engineering, with gradients of one in thirty-seven as it climbs two thousand feet through twenty-five tunnels through spurs of the mountains and across twenty-two bridges spanning ravines. In admiration of the feat and enjoyment of the scenery the human cost of the work is easily forgotten: one in three of the workers, men and women, who built the line were killed in accidents or by disease. When Kipling (ignoring the Scots, Irish and Welsh) wrote in his bombastic poem, *The English Flag*:

"For on the bones of the English
The English flag was staid..."
he forgot the Indian bones.

At Poona the news was that the 50th Indian Armoured Brigade had left for the Arakan some months previously. Since the Army seemed so inefficient, and so careless of the whereabouts of its regiments, it seemed that they would not miss me for another day, I decided to enjoy the ride down the Ghats to Bombay, see Mohan again, have a good meal and catch the overnight mail train to Calcutta, where there would be further instructions.

At the Raj Bhavan I met P C Joshi, the General Secretary of the CPI, who had been touring distant parts of the country. "P C" was a rotund and genial figure, no longer the slightly-built and hungry fugitive that he had been in the days of illegality. He urged me that, should I be in Chittagong, I was to call on his wife, Kalpana, who was in charge of the CPI centre in East Bengal (now Bangladesh).

At Victoria Terminus the booking clerk said that my pass did not entitle me to travel on the mail train, but that if I paid a few rupees more he could arrange it. On the platform the chief of train said that there were no empty second class berths, but a rupee or so later he found that there was room for me and my luggage to make the forty hour journey to Calcutta.

Even though I tried to be a "good soldier", I was not a cost effective one. The instruments (unskilfully) repaired, the batteries charged and the classes taught could not have paid for the journeys by rail, road, sea and air which I made during those two-and-a-half years, as the Army shuttled me around South East Asia. True, they allowed me to see more of India than most servicemen, but that was not what the Indian taxpayer was being made to pay for. Some of the journeying was a trial, but much of it was interesting and enjoyable.

Most of the rail journeys were on my own or with a few companions, so I was able, by cheek or *baksheesh*, to ride second class, even if the pass was third class. Most servicemen travelled in large groups in third class carriages, with wooden seats, no beds and one hole in the ground per carriage. In these they spent days and nights, cooped up, shunted into sidings, without proper catering. No wonder they detested the country. It was even worse for Indian travellers who had to fight at the stations for seats or standing room. The unlucky ones ended up sitting on windowsills, standing on the carriage steps or buffers or taking their bundles up on to the roofs. Inevitably there were accidents.

First class carriages were, by contrast, luxury caravans, comfortably furnished and equipped so that servants could prepare meals. Second class travel was not luxurious, but was comfortable and roomy. Four couchettes provided sleeping and sitting space; washing and toilet facilities were adequate. As there were no corridors or dining rooms, the trains made long stops at major stations so that travellers could buy food. Most Indians brought their own meals with them.

In such relative comfort I watched thousands of miles of Indian landscape pass: dusty, brown plains stretching away to the horizon until they met the pale blue of the sky, or muddy and forlorn under the rain; crumbling villages where women gathered at the well and small boys rode on the necks of buffaloes; rocky, scrubby jungle, palm trees and waterways. At stations and in passing towns there was all the movement and colour that Kim had watched on the Great Trunk Road; funerals with mourners dancing under umbrellas, wedding parties, religious processions, the bright saris of the women, the cloth changing in colour as one crossed the country, from the reds and blues to the white of Bengal. And there were dawns as the train crossed some great river, though in these cases the beauty was a little marred by the rows of bottoms engaged in their morning easement at the water's edge.

There were sights beside the track that were far from happy, among them the homes of the permanent way men and their families, bivouacs of straw or shacks made of tin cans and matting, homes with no kitchens or lavatories, far from water supplies, schools or medical help. I could not but compare the skinny frames of these men, who maintained the track under hot sun and monsoon rain for twelve to seventeen rupees a month with the strong limbs of the men in the gangs which worked out of Victoria and Paddington. (16 rupees then equalled £1, about £25 in today's money.) Most railway workers and their families lived in one-roomed houses built around the stations by the railway companies. Most earned less than twenty rupees a month. The lowest paid were the women who carried baskets of coal on their heads to the tenders of the locomotives for eight to ten rupees a month. The "aristocracy" was the drivers, some of whom earned up to 240 rupees a month, although most earned little more than 50 rupees. The drivers were mostly Eurasians, of whom there were colonies around the larger stations. None of the employees had unemployment, sickness or injury benefit. The railways were managed by a board appointed by the Viceroy. Its principal function was to ensure that great and guaranteed incomes were paid to the British investors. In modern values more than £7 billion were paid between 1925 and 1940.

There is something voyeuristic about travelling comfortably through a country, enjoying its sights and commenting on the poverty of its people. But my travels provided opportunities to meet and talk to Indians who were neither soldiers nor political activists. Living in a confined space with people for a day or two encourages confidences. Once, for a day and a night I travelled with an Indian family, a young husband and wife with their small son. They welcomed me and showed great kindness. We talked, their little boy played with me and they insisted on sharing their food with me. When the time came for me to change trains I thanked them sincerely, made my *nameste* and said "Perhaps we shall meet again somewhere." "Yes," replied the husband, "but you know that while you wear that uniform we can never be friends."

It was a slap, and I remembered the words of Aziz to Fielding at the end of E M Forster's *A Passage to India*:

"We shall get rid of you, yes, we shall drive every blasted Englishman into the sea. And then ... and then", he concluded, "you and I shall be friends".

10 Christmas Tea with a Heroine

Chowringhee, Calcutta's principal street, was crowded with Christmas shoppers, British and American soldiers and airmen, sahibs and memsahibs of the Raj and the well-to-do among their subjects. It was a pleasure to window-shop, to browse in a bookshop and buy a few books. I asked the proprietor what books were most bought by British servicemen. He replied, "Pornographic books".

"And by the Americans?"

"Technical books."

Just then, Indian feeling was turning against the Americans. They had been welcomed: America was not the oppressor, it proclaimed anti-colonialism, and the GIs had money to spend. But an order had gone out that no American serviceman was to marry an Indian or a Eurasian. Many young women who had been promised marriage, had liaisons or were pregnant were abandoned: it was Madam Butterfly many times over. The British, for all their arrogance, had never made such an order. Even the *Statesman* and the *Times of India* were loud in denunciation, while the popular press carried letters from betrayed women.

With evening the crowds became thicker and more animated. In the middle of it all I saw a famished looking old woman collapse on the pavement and lie with open, staring eyes while shoppers avoided her. Later, the cleansing department of the world's third largest city would collect her, and she would be included in the statistic at the bottom of a column in tomorrow's *Statesman*.

In the morning I took a train across what is now Bangladesh, a land of rivers and irrigation canals. When we came to Seri-Gunge, on the banks of the Ganges, the train could go no further. Passengers going further waited by the river or breakfasted in the cafe. After a while there arrived a double-funnelled stern wheeler, like the one in Show Boat, its paddle (in Kipling's words) chunked from Seri-Gunge to Chittagong, where I spent Christmas Eve night 1944 in a transit camp.

It was the tradition in the British Army that Christmas dinner was served by the officers to their men, as it had been in the Roman army at the mid-winter feast of Saturnalia. The dinner at Chittagong was a brave attempt at the traditional spread, but the officers were strangers to those they served.

In the afternoon I called on Kalpana Joshi, who had married P C the previous year. Kalpana was one of the heroines of the independence movement who, at the age of seventeen had been sentenced to life imprisonment on the Andaman Islands, India's "Devil's Island". When she died in 1995 her obituary in *The Guardian* said: "Before the age of twenty she had become a leader of the male-dominated revolutionary movement and a household name in Bengal". Kalpana Dutt (as she was then) had joined the Indian Republican Army and gone underground in her early teens: at seventeen she was one of a group of sixty-five revolutionaries which attacked and occupied the Chittagong police and auxilliary force armouries, raised the Indian flag and proclaimed a revolutionary government. Many of her comrades were hanged but, because of her age and gender, Kalpana was given life imprisonment. Although Gandhi disagreed with her action, he

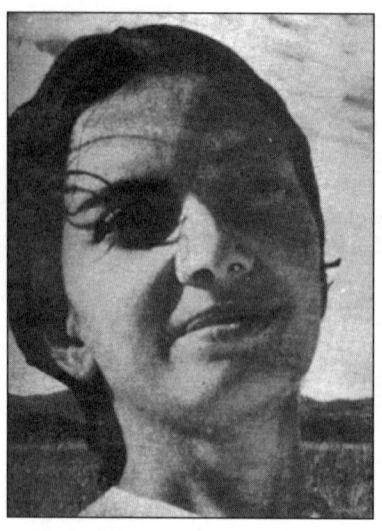

Kalpana Dutt (Joshi), former 'terrorist' with whom I had tea, Christmas Day, 1944.

visited her to show his solidarity. Public pressure secured her release after nine years. Renouncing terrorism for political action, she joined the CPI.

Some of this history I knew, but what I had not expected was to meet a gentle and beautiful woman of thirty, slightly built, with a smiling, welcoming face. After we had talked over tea, she introduced me to some of the young men and women who lived in the Chittagong commune, and left us to ask each other questions. The only question I remember was from one young woman who asked: "What does this word 'fucking' mean that we hear the soldiers saying all the time, 'the fucking this' and 'fucking that'?" My explanation raised embarrassed giggles.

From the camp I was taken to the docks to board an old tub of a ship which ran up and down the Arakan coast. We left Chittagong in darkness, and I slept on deck among the passengers, their bundles and boxes. The stars were very bright. Morning showed a world straight from Conrad, as the old ship lumbered along past villages set among coconut trees, backed by green jungle growing up the side of the mountains which divided the Arakan from Burma. From time to time passengers were dropped at little harbours.

My turn came to be landed at a jetty. In the distance the heavy guns were thumping as the Japanese were pushed out of the Arakan. While a message was sent to my unit I breakfasted at the Toc H canteen, managed by a retired officer with a military moustache. Toc H had the best canteens, which were comfortable, with food worth eating and often close to the front, in contrast to the Salvation Army for whom a cracked cup and a stale bun were good enough for "the lads".

After a time a 15 cwt. truck arrived, driven by a small, precise, dark-haired man who introduced himself as Johnnie Dance, and who drove me to the HQ Signals of the 50th Indian Armoured Brigade. It had been a long journey.

Members of the Signals Workshop in the Arakan. Author 3rd from right, the foreman and his dog on the left.

11 The Jungle and the Paddyfield

Picture a paddyfield, dry in winter, close to a dusty dirt road; through the field a stream, on one side an open space, on the other a straggle of straw buildings and mobile workshops; on three sides of the field low hills covered with scrub and pitted by dugouts; behind it the jungle, climbing up the mountains to the Nagadak Pass into Burma. This was our home and workplace.

I was introduced to a young man with sandy hair which ensured that he was called "Ginger". We were given spades and a roll of canvas and told to make ourselves a dugout. We cut a wedge in the hillside and fastened the canvas over it. Inside we could sit, but not stand, there was just room for our bedding rolls and kit. When in February, heavy rain – the *chota* (little) monsoon – sent water cascading through our home, we sat on my tin box and sang, "It ain't going to rain no more".

When the camp slept the jungle woke. The mad laugh of a hyena or the roar of something larger would be followed by the cries of monkeys and the yelping of jackals whose feet came pattering over our shelter as they ran in to scavenge around the camp. At dawn we stood outside our shelters with loaded rifles. A previous unit camped in the field had been surprised at dawn by the Japanese and all killed, except for one man who had jumped into the latrine trench.

We had such a trench - deep to keep the flies out - with a pole horizontally above it, on which one squatted. We bathed in the stream, where the trucks and jeeps were also washed, until the Foreman made baths of halves of forty gallon petrol drums so that we could have hot baths each day. For hot water, and there was usually a kettle on the go, we filled old cans with the sandy soil, impregnated the soil with petrol and set it alight. We also used petrol to wash our overalls, which should have been forbidden.

It was the Forest of Arden; my only enemy was, soon after arrival, a tummy bug and a horrible carbuncle which the MO at Brigade HQ called a "jungle sore". Otherwise life was pleasant. On new year's eve, a number of us crammed into a dugout made for four, drank and sang. One of the unit had recently died and in memory we very solemnly sang his favourite song: "You are my sunshine". One of the wireless operators (WOs) who came from near Newcastle, sang "There'll be pie in the sky when you die", because the Jarrow marchers had sung it, saying

"That such a thing could happen in a civilized country!

We'll see it doesn't happen again".

Next day, carrying rifles as ordered, three of us climbed up the *chong* (water course) into the jungle till we came to a waterfall tumbling into a pool below the pass. We stripped and jumped into water so cold that one almost blacked out and swam behind the cascade from where we could watch the colours of the jungle through the water.

Our days began with PT, then roll call (the only time we wore uniform and even then we sported a selection of hats) and breakfast, then work. Evening entertainment was sparse. Occasionally an army mobile cinema came to Brigade HQ, a large screen was set up in the open air, and we sat in rows to watch; officers in front, then British troops, then Indian. Once an ENSA company brought Agatha Christie's *Ten Little Nigger Boys*, as it was then called. But we had an officially-sponsored discussion group which met three evenings a week. Topics varied from films and film stars to the situation in Greece and the future of Germany. I opened once on "Shall we be richer or poorer after the war?" and another time on the Beveridge Report, for which we divided into two groups, one side being the Cabinet and the other the General Council of the TUC. There was a mock trial in which I had to defend the Foreman, who had killed his wife because she was in pain with incurable cancer. A speaker on "Should transport be nationalised?", was in favour of private enterprise, but the audience was not. An officer from the Brigade, who had been in the CID Vice Squad told us of some of the bizarre goings-on in the West End.

These discussions continued during our work; the atmosphere in the Squadron was quite political. The Foreman of Signals,[8] known as "Mush", was a Labour Party activist from Hornsey. Two other left Labour people were Lievesley, from Rossington in the Yorkshire coalfield, and "Taffy", a North Wales quarry worker who had become a Liverpool policeman because of unemployment. Both became my friends, and after the war I spent a weekend with Lievesley and his family, and they took me for a walk in the rhubarb fields. There were two Welsh ex-miners to help keep the left bias. We had only two firm and articulate Tories: Johnnie Dance was a pleasant but very conventional assistant head of a technical school in Birmingham, and a farmer's son. He was an old time rural Tory, but was willing to discuss. The other, whom I shall call "Walls" (he claimed to have been the transport manager for Walls Ice Cream, but had probably been a junior in that department) was a rather unpleasant proto-Thatcherite.

One of the major comforts of our life was that we ate well, better than our officers. Bill, our Sergeant cook, and the cornerstone of the squadron, had been manager of the Westminster Bank at Exmouth, and continued to draw his salary in the army; he put his army pay into a kitty, to which we all contributed a percentage of our pay. With this fund he added to army rations by visiting villages and bazaars to buy chicken, eggs and fresh vegetables.

Helping Bill were, Munga, Dunda and Bul Singh. Munga was portly and would stand with a ladle calling, "Come along, *khanna* (food) up"'. Dunda, thin and quick, was a skilled conjuror. One evening he arranged an entertainment for us, with comic patter, in which people found eggs appearing in their pockets and handkerchiefs materialising out of the air. Munga and Dunda were - nominally - Christians. Bul Singh was a fifteen year old whom Bill had rescued from a circus - a waif who had earned a pittance as a clown. Now, well fed and wearing a uniform too big for him, he still had the gait and mock seriousness of a clown. When a troupe of Indian dancers came to entertain us, Bul Singh was so excited by a pretty young girl that he gave her all his money and his watch to go on dancing, while he trembled with desire. He looked on Bill as his father and called him *Baba*. He said he would go to England with Bill, but never could.

31

12 Messengers of the Gods?

Mercury, symbol of the Royal Corps of Signals, carried messages for the Gods. Our, less exalted, task was to keep messages flowing between the Brigadier and his staff, whom we never saw, and our three battalions who were engaged against the Japanese somewhere to the south and east. As was usual in the Indian Army, two of the battalions were of Indian troops and one of British. Two were called "cavalry" and one "lancers" although there were neither horses nor lances. The British, the 146 Cavalry something, had an anthem beginning "We are the ek, char, chey (one four six)", and a song:

"Mosquitoes, bugs and flies,
Tear out your bleeding eyes,
Roll on the boat that takes us home".

The messages were passed by mobile radio stations on beaches, islands and mountain tops within a twenty mile radius. The "ops" would return with "duff" radios or exhausted batteries, rest a few days, and disappear somewhere else. Occasionally they would send a message asking the workshop for help and one of us would go out. Not long after my arrival Cpl. Shepherd drove me in a jeep up the mule track, along vertiginous edges above the treetops to the Nagadak pass.

Then the Foreman asked me to visit a station on a beach twenty miles up the coast, and do a repair or exchange the set. It was a pleasant duty, driving past villages among coconut palms bending in the wind and curious children staring as I went by, and always the sea was on one side and the mountains and the jungle on the other. From time to time *chongs* cut across the road, bridged by two railway sleepers just the width of the jeep's wheel-base, over which I crept. My goal was idyllic, miles of sandy beach, blue sea and palms; and after a minor repair and a meal with the "ops", a leisurely drive home.

There were some eight of us in the workshop. Mush was the most respected person in the squadron, easy to like, a good craftsman and a socialist. He was always accompanied by his dog. When he left India he shot the dog at the dockside because he could not bear the thought of it becoming a stray. What he missed most was his Sunday cycle run. Corporal Shepherd had owned a wireless shop. He enjoyed physical activity and when on leave rode in the Himalayas. I remember him dancing round the paddyfield holding the dog in his arms like a baby. The rest of us were Lance Corporals, Johnnie Dance, Ginger, my tent mate, Taffy the Liverpool copper, Lievesley, myself, and an unpleasant young man, a pathological racist whose every second word was "fucking".

There was also Sammy Goldberg, who looked like all those cartoons of Jews in Julius Streicher's Nazi periodical *Der Stuermer*. He was a delightful colleague, with a store of self-deprecatory Jewish jokes and a uniform that fell about him like Schweik's. But poor Sammy was accident prone. His bad eyesight and thick glasses should have kept him out of the army. He managed to cascade the Foreman's tea all over himself and to sit in someone's dinner. One morning, arriving late on parade, he tripped and rolled down the hillside on to the parade ground. The end was catastrophe. One day the kettle was boiling slowly; Sammy poured petrol on to the fire, set himself alight and had to be rushed to hospital. We did not see him again.

Our other casualty deserved what he got. He was an unpleasant Sergeant, with a whine in his Liverpool accent, who announced that he would get out of the army by faking a breakdown. So he started tearing up pieces of paper and was sent to a mental hospital in Deolali ("to go Doolally" was slang for to go mad). The Indian troops said his madness was because he had killed a monkey. The Foreman told me that the Sergeant had wanted a young pet monkey so, seeing a mother monkey with a baby he had shot and wounded her. She fell from the tree and he seized the baby. The mother crawled towards him, holding out her hands and crying. He shot her. The baby died. To the Indians he was doomed.

There were thirty to forty Indian troops working with us, mostly young Muslims from the Punjab. Their Mullah was a bearded truck driver. A few were ops, one or two were with the workshop, but most of them were drivers or were maintaining vehicles. There was only the one extreme racist among us. The general attitude, based on small experience and extensive ignorance, was; "They're OK in their way. Some are good chaps, but most are lazy bastards. They're no good at anything mechanical and you can't teach them. If India were independent there would be a terrible balls-up. But let them have it, then we can go home." There was no mixing between British and Indians, except at work.

Our racist was in charge of the battery shop, where he vented his spleen on his assistant, Wali Mahommed, a gentle young man with no enthusiasm for the army, who infuriated the racist with "*malum nai*" (I don't understand) or, "*tora pichi*" (the equivalent of "*mañana*"). There were also two Eurasians, who ranked as British. One was quite happy, but the other hated not being "white", so much so that when his mother sent him a parcel, he returned it unopened because of his resentment against her for her Indian skin.

We hardly ever saw our "superiors". The Sergeant Major, a weak character, scarcely ever came out of his office. The Major was waiting to retire after a lifetime in the Indian Army. The Captain was a fussy, cocky, Jewish solicitor from Liverpool, something of a joke to both British and Indians. At my first meal after arrival, he asked in the mess, "Who is this man Fyrth? I've got instructions to censor all his mail carefully." Later he said to me: "Your letters are the most interesting I have to read. Where do you get all this information?"

He decided that we should run before breakfast, instead of having PT. The first morning we dutifully obeyed. Thereafter, led by Cpl. Shepherd, we ran out of camp to a quarry round the corner, sat down for a smoke and puffed back into camp. But one morning, as we sat down, the Captain came round the corner in his running shorts. We were made to parade after work in full kit and march up and down the paddyfield for half-an-hour, to the amusement of the Indians. But there was no more running.

By March 1945 the Brigade was no longer wanted in the Arakan. We packed up, drove to Chittagong and took the boat to Madras.

13 Land, Lots of Land

Madras was a shock, a tropcal city, humid, alive with colour, noise and crowded streets. It was a relief to head into the countryside, north-westward towards Ahmednagar, seven hundred miles away. We were four days on the road; the British Other Ranks, led by the Foreman in his mobile workshop; the rest of us two by two in jeeps and trucks. The officers had left us at Madras and re-appeared at Ahmednagar. When we met officers of other units they shook their heads at the idea of two dozen men with fifteen or so vehicles crossing India without the benefit of officers. The Indians had their own convoy and we did not see them on the journey. Bill and Bul Singh went ahead with the mobile kitchen and Munga and Danda followed in the water wagon. They stopped in villages to buy food so that each evening when we came into harbour they had a good hot meal waiting for us.

After fifty years there remains a memory of heat and dust. The dust we stirred up from the white roads, and the heat overcame us, so that I found myself bumping across a field as I drowsed over the wheel. We assuaged the heat with ice-cold water from our *chagals*, canvas bottles shaped like the goatskins from which they were descended. We tied them to the front of our radiators, so that the sun and the engines evaporated the surface water leaving it cold. With "Carnation" tinned milk it was delicious.

My jeep mate, a young wireless op, had acquired a small, yellow-brown, pyard puppy. As we passed an elephant with the mahout sitting on its neck, the puppy was panic stricken and yelped hysterically at the great beast, which, in turn, released its breakfast in the road, an awesome sight at close quarters.

One evening, in a Deccan town, the Foreman took to few of us to meet a rather world-weary English businessman he knew, who declared that he did not intend to stay on after independence because everything would be such a mess.

Another night we camped by a lake, sat round fires and slept on the ground or in the backs of trucks. The sky was deep blue and the stars very bright. The Deccan stretched for many miles and quiet voices sang:

"Give me land lots of land and the starry sky above,
Don't fence me in."

Next day we drove into the great fort at Ahmednagar.

14 Chand Bibi's Fort

The fort, like a Norman castle, was a fortified area of open spaces and buildings, among which were the huts in which we lived and worked. On a parade ground in front of our huts was a standing tap, where crows, mynah birds and robins came to drink. The Indian robins were the size of thrushes, and had red backsides, not breasts. The walls were impressive, about twenty-five feet high and wide enough for three people to walk abreast, enjoy an evening stroll and look at the surrounding countryside.

The fort was part of the tangle of Indian history. Built in 1550 at the centre of an independent Muslim state, it was conquered fifty years later by Akbar, founder of the Moghul Empire. It passed backwards and forwards between different Empires, and at one time was held by an African slave, who rose to be Chief Minister and kept the Moghuls at bay. In the mid seventeenth century the area was swept by famine; much of it lay waste for twenty five years until repopulated from outside. After the death of Aurangzeb, the last great Moghul, it became part of the Maratha kingdom which dominated western India. From the Marathas it was seized by an East India Company army led by the future Duke of Wellington. On top of the wall was a plaque which read:

"On this spot General Arthur Wellesley took
his breakfast after defeating the army of
Chand Bibi on August 12th 1803."

I hoped that Sir Arthur enjoyed sharing his breakfast with the vultures and jackals feasting on the remains of his soldiers, and those of the Maratha queen.

The traces of these ancient glories were scattered around the poverty stricken countryside. Were the peasants living in the ruins of large stone buildings too poor to wonder about their history?

When we arrived, in March 1945, the fort was still at the centre of Indian history; it was the prison of Jawaharlal Nehru and the leaders of the Congress Party, who had been there since the "Quit India" call of 1942, when they had been arrested. One afternoon Wali Mahommed said to me: "We are going to see Mr Nehru this evening; have you got a message you would like to send him?" I sent one of general good wishes.

I had inherited the battery shop, which did essential but not technically difficult work, and Wali was my assistant. We got on well together; he was a gentle young man with a sense of humour and a disrespect for authority. Like most of his fellow soldiers, he spoke English fluently, although there were some British who insisted on speaking bastard Hindustani to them.

As the flat batteries came in from radios and vehicles we lifted them on to wooden benches: it was forbidden for one man to lift them on his own. We cleaned them, topped them up with diluted acid, put them on charge and checked them from time to time. Two large charging engines and two small "chore horses" had to be kept clean and full of petrol and oil. The engines had to be kept going day and night when necessary. The job allowed plenty of time for reading and writing – no smoking – and chatting to passers by who dropped in. Wali asked me for books and I lent him some about India and some about the Muslim republics of the Soviet Union.

Not all the sepoys were as gentle as Wali. There was a large, handsome, wild Pathan from the Frontier who was exchanging looks with one of a group of women working on the paths of the fort. He picked her up and carried her to his billet. The villainous contractor in charge of the women demanded that the Pathan pay him money; the CO, justly, said that the money should go to the woman. The next day I saw her smiling when the Pathan passed.

There had been changes: the Major had gone into his retirement and had been replaced by a Major whom we called the "Tailor's Dummy", because he looked like the wax figures in the window of Burton's before the war. The Liverpool solicitor had also disappeared and when a pleasant and competent Captain arrived we gave him a party. Making a speech of welcome, Johnnie Dance announced that "The motto of this unit is, technical efficiency first and to hell with bullshit!"

The look on the Captain's face was one of some astonishment. He had us doing drill each morning after that.

Because the squadron had been some time in the Arakan everyone was given twenty-eight days leave. I chose to take mine in Bombay, when my turn came at the end of March.

15 Bombay Spring

My notebooks record the rumblings of the volcano that could be heard that spring beneath the surface of Bombay. But that spring was also enjoyable.

Those who had chosen to go to Bombay included Bill, the cook, and Ginger, my former tent mate. We stayed in a boarding house kept by a young middle-aged English widow, who had none of the characteristics of a memsahib, indeed could have kept a lodging house at any English resort. She provided us with comfortable beds and English breakfasts. One evening I returned to find Bill chasing her round the dining room table; both were in their underclothes and Bill was shouting, "We're all made the same way", though that did not seem to be what he was trying to prove.

My recollections are of the pleasures of Breach Candy, a luxurious swimming pool of warm sea water, in which to float and see the vultures sailing over the Parsee Tower of Silence. The pool was strictly "apartheid". I could have taken in my dog, had I had one, but not an Indian friend. It was said that the doorman could tell if a soldier's girl-friend had the slightest drop of Indian blood.

When I arrived at the Raj Bhavan, Mohan said, "There's an English Captain here who I know you would like to meet." In the bookshop was "Push" - Izzy Pushkin, who introduced himself as from East London, where he had taken part in the struggle against the Blackshirts and had been involved in the tenants' movements of the 1930s. He had served in the Buffs but had transferred to the Army Education Corps and was teaching in the formation college at Poona, to which he was about to return.

After the war we were colleagues at work and lifelong friends. In India we met whenever we could. On one occasion I was in Bombay on a 48 hour pass and he on a longer leave. He decided we should have a week together, so phoned my CO and arranged it. Both of us remembered that week, talking late as we sat on the sea wall. We met a sorry group of deserters by the Gateway to India: how did they live? The officer among them claimed it was by selling his sexual favours: how did they hope ever to return to England? We recalled bundling a scatter-brained Major on to his train, having seen he was fed and packed, and then collapsing in laughter.

One sad morning all the flags were at half-mast for Roosevelt. I felt apprehension for the future. An American serviceman had told us, "Look out for his Vice-President. He's connected with the Pendergast mob." (When Pendergast died President Truman attended his funeral saying, "He was my friend".) Roosevelt was very popular in India, as was Stalin. Both were regarded as anti-colonialists and both seen as progressives in social matters. Stalin's crimes were then not known, although there were some who did condemn him. I recall Mohan saying, "When I hear condemnation of Soviet actions I ask myself whether I or any of my comrades would be guilty of such deeds and think that we wouldn't, so probably such stories are untrue." Unfortunately the logic of his argument was false.

I had chosen Bombay for leave hoping to learn more of Indian conditions. The CPI was then influential in Bombay, so Mohan was able to arrange me a programme of visits and discussions with people in politics, education and culture. These people were very willing to express their views to a "non-official Englishman". I also spent time studying documents, books and journals about various people's movements, trade unions, women's movements, students' organisations, the *kisan sababs* (peasant leagues), about caste and untouchability and about unrest among the people. All these I discussed with Mohan and party leaders as well as with Congress members and others.

16 A People Going to Pieces

"The people are going to pieces. After the famine came the epidemics. Three million people have died. Now there is a complete collapse of morality." This was Mohan in our first discussion. Villages in Bengal, he said, were deserted, paddies unplanted, artisans ruined, rural education had collapsed. Corruption and prostitution were rife, thousands of women were destitute and higher caste women who engaged in relief work were looked on as prostitutes. Congress and the Muslim League were riven with divisions.

Now there was a cloth famine. Two dhotis and a sari cost a month's wages, but cloth was usually unavailable on the open market, and on the black market it cost twice as much. As soon as cloth appeared in the approved shops it was bought by hoarders and sold on the black market. Thousands of looms were idle because weavers could not get yarn. Only in Bengal, where a progressive alliance had overthrown the provincial government, was there any effective control.

I went to a meeting about the shortage. About 250 middle class people listened to speakers, women, students, trade unionists and a merchant. Ranadive, speaking for the Communist Party, began: "There is also a famine in honesty", and attacked the triangle of millionaires, hoarders and government. He also attacked the citizens of Bombay for not supporting textile workers who were campaigning for improved living standards without going on strike. The audience passed a resolution supporting an anti-hoarding drive, democratically controlled rationing of cloth and better conditions for textile workers.

At a meeting of the Textile Workers' Union I saw the hand-made posters which had won them a campaign. The mother of a millionaire had promised at *Puja* (purification prayer) that each worker should be given a sari or a dhoti. But her son had broken the promise. A two-week campaign with posters had made him keep the promise.

As people left the villages the population of Bombay had grown by two-thirds. The military had meanwhile requisitioned a number of houses. The city engineer said that ten people now lived on average in each Bombay room: but that 200,000 were homeless. Every night families slept in doorways and passages or in the streets with their belongings beside them. A room required an extortionate rent and a bribe of four to five hundred rupees. (16 rupees equalled £1).

A milk shortage had followed the growth of population; the price had risen eighteen fold. Under pressure from women's organisations, Bombay City Government had banned the use of fresh milk in cafes and hotels, and had subsidised milk for mothers and children, saying that only when their demand was met could milk be sold. The merchants had replied by pouring 300,000 gallons into the gutters.

17 Rumblings

It was no surprise to hear the rumblings of revolt in Bombay. Soon after I arrived there was a general strike in the city. Eight people who had taken part in the 1942 riots were to be hanged. Gandhi called for prayer for a miracle and for a *hartel* (closing of shops and businesses). I saw a third to a half of the shops shut in a lower middle class area and heard that all were closed in the working class districts. The Communist Party called for a general strike, except in transport and public utilities. This would counter demoralisation and show that the CPI was united with Congress in the national struggle. In response between two and three hundred thousand workers came out, including most of the textile workers.

I travelled in a rickety CPI bus to a textile mill area. All the mills were shut, with workers guarding their gates. Some twenty five thousand workers, Hindu and Moslem, men and women were sitting on the *Kangar Maidan* (workers' open space). Those around asked who I was and were delighted when told. They offered to translate for me, and when I said something about the language always being the same in workers' struggles, were even more pleased. The crowd was disciplined and clearly accepted the authority of the party speakers. During the speeches news arrived that the executions had been stayed and the crowd burst into cheers.

Next morning the strikers went back, but when a group started throwing stones and breaking windows eight mills stopped work. The party rushed out a leaflet saying "go back and produce cloth to end the famine". They went back.

After the strike meeting I walked back to our lodgings through a crowd of drunken servicemen, pimps and hawkers in the "leave quarter". Bill said that he had seen a drunken sailor dancing naked on a table in the Prince of Wales, the servicemen's pub.

Three days later the railways struck. On the protest day they had stopped for ten minutes by agreement between the union secretary and the railway director. But the secretary had been arrested by the government for issuing a leaflet. There was a spontaneous strike of railway and bus workers. Forty union officials were arrested and services in central Bombay manned by servicemen and volunteers. In outer areas there was a standstill. To break the impasse, S K Patil, the Congress boss in Bombay, ended the strike with a compromise. The union leaders were released and the company allowed to victimise twenty-five workers of its own choosing. There was confusion as Congress supported the deal, the CPI opposed it and the Congress Socialist Party called for more militant action. Some workers stayed out, some went back unwillingly.

As my leave came to an end preparations were being made all over the city to celebrate May Day, and I heard the *International* being sung in Hindi.

18 Barefoot Doctors

Dr Basu was an eminent Bengali medical man who in 1937 had been sent by Nehru, as one of five doctors in a Congress medical mission, to Mao and the Chinese Eighth Route Army fighting against the Japanese. With lessons he had learned in China, he had returned to Bengal to head the medical board of the People's Relief Committee in the wake of famine and epidemics. The PRC had been formed because the government was doing so little, and was made up of representatives of Congress, Muslim League, CPI, Bengal trade unions, student and women's organisations, together with Indian People's Theatre and the Anti-fascist Writers and Artists Association. The cultural groups toured the country raising funds.

Basu was in Bombay for a few days and I was lucky to have a long conversation with him. A few days later he invited me with Mohan and Krishnan, Mohan's brother-in-law, to join him and a young Chinese woman in a "real Chinese meal".

In our talk, Basu told me that the PRC medical board had treated 2,200,000 patients in one year compared with 100,000 treated at ten times cost per head by the government campaign. At first the medical board had only five doctors: they had divided Bengal into regions and each had built up ninety units of volunteers. Some of these were British Quakers and some American Quakers: the Society of Friends had sent money. They had trained village boys to go round the countryside giving anti-malarial inoculations and quinine pills. As soon as a unit visited an area it was swamped with patients who had walked ten or fifteen miles from surrounding villages. There were always two, three or four hundred waiting for treatment so the volunteers were terribly overworked.

I asked what were the main obstacles to medical work in India; he replied lack of personnel. There were only 400,000 doctors in India; many were in the army, most in the towns. And there was only about one nurse to forty doctors. So villages had no medical staff but plenty of quacks. There was great prejudice against women becoming nurses, as it was believed that nurses were forced to become unchaste. Drugs were short and India had no drug industry. There was a large black market in drugs and controls were in the hands of importing companies, who also ran the black market.

Preventative medicine was almost impossible because the clearing of irrigation ditches, clean water and drainage were in the hands of central government which did almost nothing. The Department of Health was part of a ministry dealing with many topics and was neglected. During the worst of the epidemics the Army had given great help, releasing doctors, setting up hospitals and giving inoculations. But as the situation had eased, though it was still bad, that help had been withdrawn.

Was there any opposition to their medical work? I asked. Yes, both Hindu and Muslim superstitions were against inoculations, and especially against vaccinations. Opposition had been made worse by forced vaccination in official centres, and these were often met by force. Some of the lymph had been useless and those vaccinated had died of smallpox, but the medical board had successfully overcome prejudices and fears.

Had they found that the traditional ayurvedic medicine was of use? He wished that there had been more research into the value of traditional remedies. With such a shortage of western drugs many ayurvedic drugs had been found valuable, but research was needed to decide on the correct amounts to use. Such research and analysis as had been done was showing the true value. In China research had been carried out into their traditional methods and proving the worth of such remedies. The Eighth Route Army received so few western drugs that it was necessary to rely heavily on traditional methods. He told me how, during the Chinese Red Army's Long March[9] a class of 150 medical students had been trained, and how specimens for study had been passed back along the ranks while they were on the march.

I asked what was now needed in Bengal and he replied that at first the relief work was urgent, but that now it had to be backed up by rehabilitation. Agriculture must be rebuilt, irrigation restored and anti-malarial precautions taken. The PRC units were working on such a programme, but government action was needed urgently.

19 Looking for Answers

Doctor Adhikari explained to me the economic background to the tide of misery engulfing the country. India had been used as a base against the Japanese, but there had been no or very little, expansion of Indian production. Instead, British and American Lend-Lease goods had been imported for the war effort. These had been paid for with paper money backed by frozen sterling balances held in London. The result had been inflation with its attendant hoarding, profiteering, black markets and corruption. The government had not stamped on these, so strikes occurred which had reduced coal output and so cut textile output.

Looking for economic solutions, I paid three visits to the Bombay School of Economics, a post-graduate institution with excellent research and library facilities, for long discussions with staff and students. But the staff wanted me to tell them about the British government's wartime economic strategy, about the Cambridge economics of Keynes and about the Beveridge Report, while I wanted them to talk about India.

The lecturer with whom I had the longest discussion had a full grasp of India's problems, and was full of ideas for solutions, but was depressed, as were all others I met, about the political future, seeing no hope of a lead from either India or Britain. He saw repression growing worse as soldiers going home painted a false picture of an India which they had not really seen. He was left-wing Congress, read *People's War*, but was critical of the CPI, to which he had been close until August 1942.

Two students whom I met were extremely nationalistic, following Nehru and Azad (the President of Congress), and seeing the way to liberation through the organisation of peasants, workers and students. They saw the CPI as the best organiser of these three, but thought it divisive, for supporting the Tata-Birla Plan (the detailed economic plan for the industrialisation of India, issued in the name of the two leading capitalists), and for supporting the nationalisation plan of the government's Economic Planning Committee – an idea then in the news. These plans meant cooperation with the government, which the Indian people would never accept. The Communists followed an international line and ignored the national interests and the psychology of the Indian people. One of these students was studying land tenure and the other currency movements. BV Krishna Murthy, with whom I also had a discussion, was a left-wing economist at the School. Although he thought it strange that the government was proposing nationalisation, he said that the best economic brains in India had been taken into the Planning Department and these wanted nationalisation, while the government saw such a step as the best way for it to keep control of the economy and to exclude the USA, while at the same time harming the Indian capitalists. He himself thought the nationalisation policy should be supported because it would weaken the hold of the capitalists on the Congress Party and so make the task of a national government easier. It would also make more difficult an alliance of the Indian capitalists with either their British or American counterparts. But any support for nationalisation should be backed with demands for a national government, trade union representation and joint production committees in industry and democratic planning machinery.

These discussions made me feel that India had good economists, from whom much was to be hoped. But that everything would depend on independence and the establishment of a national government.

20 One Nation or Two?

That spring in Bombay it seemed impossible that India could be denied independence, even though Churchill was opposed and the Labour Party divided. But would it be as one nation or two?[10]

I had accepted the Congress view, that India was one nation and any talk of a Muslim state (Pakistan) was divisive and exploited by the Raj. But that April I learned that the problem was more complex. It is easier now to see the mistakes that were made in the partition of 1948 and the horrors that followed – massacres, two wars and religious fundamentalism in both India and Pakistan. For these no party or group, including the British, is free from blame, but some carry more responsibility than others.

But in the spring of 1945 all that was in the future. I had a long conversation with the CPI General Secretary P C Joshi who said the British government must first free all political prisoners and then set up a national government of India. Mohan's view was that such a government should consist of equal representation of Congress and Muslim League with one Sikh, one Parsee, one Christian and possibly representatives of Dr Ambedkhar's organisation of *harijans* (untouchables). This national government should declare independence and begin negotiation on details. There should be no insistence on either Pakistan or no-Pakistan before independence, that was for the Indian parties to sort out themselves. The same view was being propagated by Mrs Naidu, the leading woman in Congress.

But what was Pakistan? No one seemed to know. Even Jinnah was not adamant that it meant a separate state. At Ahmedabad in 1935 he had been vague. It meant to obtain the liberation of all India; it meant a united front which would force the British to disengage. It meant freedom for India. It would be a democratic state in which minorities would get a square deal – meanwhile all communities should work together to improve the position of the poor.

Now in 1945, did it mean cultural autonomy for Muslim areas? Or home rule in Muslim majority states (or areas?) within a federal India? Or did it mean complete independence? And if so, would it be a Muslim or a secular state? And would Bengal (or at least Eastern Bengal) be part of Pakistan, even though a thousand miles from the Muslim areas of the Punjab and the

North-West? The idea of "The Land of the Pure" had gradually taken shape in the 1920-30s, but it was the war which proved the catalyst. A document drawn up after the breakdown of talks between Gandhi and Jinnah in September 1944 told me something of the history of Hindu-Muslim relations during the 20th century and especially since the elections of 1937 in which Congress won a majority (on a complicated voting system) and formed governments in six provinces. These governments introduced important social reforms, but also perpetrated wrongs against Muslims; all children were to be taught in Hindi, so discriminating against the Muslim Urdu speakers. Congress flags were to fly over schools and be saluted as though they were national flags, and so on.

In 1939 Congress ministers resigned in protest at India being declared at war without consultation with the Indian people. Ministers were arrested; so were national leaders such as Nehru. When they declared civil disobedience, 100,000 people went into concentration camps. When in 1942 the proposals brought by Stafford Cripps were rejected by the Indian parties, turmoil followed. The conventional view is that Congress launched civil disobedience and demanded that the British quit India: it was less simple. The Japanese were already in Assam, and when the All India Central Committee of Congress met in Bombay there were clashes among its leaders. Azad, the President, was rousingly patriotic and anti-Japanese; Nehru was anti-Japanese and was organising a People's Defence Force, but was angry with the British; Patel, the iron head of party organisation, said "We cannot trust the British to defend India, so they must go". Gandhi was confused and pacifist; the Congress Socialist Party wanted an immediate uprising; the Communists called for Congress-League unity and a "people's war" against Japan. The Nehru-Azad line prevailed – the government should be asked to negotiate; civil disobedience if it refused. The government immediately arrested the leaders and cut them off from news for three years. Meetings were banned. Leaderless or CSP-inspired attacks followed.

The Congress Socialist Party stepped into the vacuum and took on leadership in some areas. But where peasant leagues or trade union organisation was strong, or where the CPI had strong influence, there were peaceful protests not riots – though sometimes the protests were attacked by police. The government clamped down with mass arrests, floggings and burning of villages where there was trouble. Many Congressmen and some Communists were arrested, some shot.

So throughout the war the Muslim League made the running in political propaganda and was naturally favoured by the British because of its support of the war and because of the important role of Muslim troops. By 1945 most Muslims no longer saw Congress as a national party – to them it was a Hindu party, with a few Muslim members. A united India would mean Hindu rule. To Congress the League was a separatist body. In 1944, when Gandhi was released because of his wife's death, he and Jinnah met to discuss an agreement, but failed to reconcile their opposing conceptions of freedom for India. The result was to widen the breach between Hindus and Muslims. Joshi said there had always been a communal trend in Congress: now it was speaking up boldly and overtures were being made to the extremist Hindu *Mahasabah*. Muslims were leaving Congress and Communists being pushed out. There were growing clashes between the two communities.

It was in this context that in 1943 Chakravarti Rajagopalichari, the popular Congress leader in South India who later was the first Governor General of independent India, put forward a compromise proposal. There should be a plebiscite in all Muslim majority areas to see whether they wished to separate from India. Both Gandhi and Jinnah made sympathetic noises, and then attacked the idea. Many in Congress and the CPI saw the idea as a way out, but thought Indian independence and a national government would have to come first. It was argued that Muslims were now becoming a separate nation within India and should have the right of self-determination. In India, unlike Europe, religion and culture and sometimes language were inseparable from a sense of nationhood and must be part of the definition of a "nation".

Not everyone accepted this theory. A paper in the CPI records by Dr S V Ansari, a Muslim, argued the traditional case. India was geographically and economically one; everyone had become "Indianised" in the struggle with Britain. The "two nation" theory had grown only out of the political conflicts of the war years. Hindus had treated Muslims as untouchables and were economically exclusive, but a theory could not be based on middle class differences. Pakistan was not properly defined; it would not help Muslims in Hindu areas. The masses needed socialism not nationalism. A separate Pakistan would be poor in resources and (prophetically) there could be war between the two states.

21 Discordant Voices

I met some of the key political players in Bombay. K A Abbas was one of India's leading journalists, a Muslim socialist, a member of Congress and a rationalist. We met in the office of the *Bombay Chronicle*. We discussed

Viceroy Wavell's strategy of economic advance, by-passing independence, and Beverley Nichols' book *Verdict on India*, of which he said that Nichols was escorted everywhere by government representatives and had given a false picture of what he had seen.

Although Abbas disagreed with the Communists, he admired them for trying to rouse the people to fight cloth shortages, epidemics and famines, and agreed that nationalists took the attitude that nothing could be done because they were not in power, but he stressed that I must understand the psychology of the Indians. They were frustrated, so suspicious of the government and the bureaucracy that they would not co-operate with authority. He himself was frustrated but did not know what to do. The CPI's "people's war" slogan took no account of the psychology of the Indian masses, who saw the party as standing aloof from the independence struggle in 1942, and while the war might benefit India in the long run the majority of Indians could not be expected to see that. Talk of self-determination for Muslims or of Pakistan gave the Muslim League an ideological cover. Self-determination would have to be granted to many areas, not only Muslim, but should not be based on religious grounds. Congress-League unity was not possible because with every concession Jinnah raised his demands. Unity was fruitless because the League had no anti-imperialist tradition. It was based on religious fanaticism. Jinnah's aim was power for himself and his party. Of course, Congress was also partly to blame: it included strands of Hindu revivalism and capitalist influences and these should be purged. He ended with a plea for a "psychological" approach to the problems of India.

The message at the provincial office of the Muslim League was very different. Mr Sheikh and Jussef Moliduna, the joint secretaries, were young and liberal-minded, and anxious to make the League democratic. They denied that the claim of Muslims to be a nation was based on religion alone but on languages, cultures and ways of life, unlike the Catholic-Protestant divide in Europe, where, they said, differences could be forgotten outside the church. Hindus and Muslims were more different than the English and French, and Muslims in Bengal, for instance, had more in common with Muslims in Madras than with their Hindu neighbours who treated them as another people.

Then why not have provincial autonomy? Because the most important matters would be in Hindu hands at the centre. In Pakistan provinces that wished to secede would be given that right. The people would decide whether Pakistan would be a theocratic or secular state. Boundary changes in the Punjab and Assam would be made by agreement, but Calcutta would be vital to East Pakistan.

They would not admit to corruption in the League administration or League ministries. Nor that Pakistan would be economically weak or used as a wedge by the British, like Ulster. Their picture of the way forward was through Congress-League unity, which should be possible if the CPI used its influence where it was strong.

The chance of such unity seemed remote when I met S K Patil, the Congress leader in Bombay and on the City Corporation. Patil, a tough little Gujerati bureaucrat and a very capable organiser, had been Mayor of Bombay and had had his share of prison. He was very anti-Communist and had played a major part in re-orientating Congress to become a monolithic party. He had spent some years in England and had studied at the LSE, where he had been greatly influenced, he said, by Harold Laski.

He was not against Pakistan, but it would have to be after the declaration of independence when Congress-League agreement would be reached within 24 hours. It would have to be settled in accordance with Gandhi's idea, agreed to – he claimed – by 90% of Congress, of "brothers parting as friends". But most of Bengal and the North West Frontier Province did not want Pakistan and Jinnah had been intransigent since the Cripps mission of 1942. However, when I asked him how India could become independent when it was divided, he snapped at me, "How dare you speak of division when your country has created and fostered every division in the land?"

We turned to other matters. India, he said, would gain nothing from the war and had nothing to hope from a Labour government. India must stand on its own feet. I asked about untouchability. It was "a minor problem", not accepted by 90% of Hindus. Dr Ambedkhar, leader of the *Harijans*, was "a charlatan". Like other internal problems, it could be dealt with only after independence. Nothing much could be done against famine, disease and illiteracy until Indians were free. Corruption and the black market were protected and encouraged by the British. Protests at the cloth famine all went into the waste paper basket (he made a gesture towards his own). Freedom would give a surge of enthusiasm. Bringing our meeting to an end, he said England should realise that there would be gains on both sides economically and from cultural ties and British medical advance. (Mohan said this was not his usual line.) He had no ill will against the English, on the contrary he admired their initiative and discipline. I and my fellow servicemen should tell people at home the facts of India as we had seen them.

Looking back, already in 1945 the division of India was probably inevitable. And conflict was very probable. The way these negotiations were carried out and the decisions implemented made both certain. At that time everyone gravely underestimated the importance and danger of both Muslim and Hindu fundamentalism.

22 A Visit to the Mahatma

One morning Mohan said, "Why don't you go and see the Old Man? He's very accessible. Only watch out for his secretary, Pyeralal. He stops anyone whose ideas he thinks bad for the Old Man." We had been discussing Gandhi, who was staying at Birla House, the home of the millionaire Birla, on Malabar Hill, for talks with Congress leaders.

Congress Party contained rival groups – some to the left, others on the right. They would all come to Gandhi with their opinions; he would listen and then come out with a solution that would satisfy them all. We did not know that this time he was going to fail. Mohan told me of meeting peasants who had told him that Gandhi had made them conscious that they were Indians. That was the source of his influence.

He was also capable of nonsense. A few weeks earlier he had issued a condemnation of the CPI on the grounds that, he had been told, it encouraged its followers to eat meat, and that members held their wives in common, as advocated by one of its writers, Frederick Engels, in a book called *The Origin of the Family*. At a crucial moment in the discussions on independence, in 1946-47, he asked the government to ban horse racing, because the poor lost their money in betting. Now his entourage was doing what it could to isolate him from any view favouring Pakistan.

"You might," said Mohan, "be able to glean some idea as to the way he is thinking." I took the bus to Malabar Hill and walked between the palaces on each side of the road, the huge block of the Sassoons, the international bankers, and Jinnah's palace, built in 1930's Odeon-Moghul style. At Birla House my name was taken by teenage Congress Volunteers in their "Gandhi Caps" and I was asked to wait in a reception room. That afternoon Gandhi was in discussion with Abdul Gaffir Khan, leader of Congress Red Shirts in the North West Province, and known as the Frontier Gandhi on account of his pacifism. He had just been released from prison. His bodyguard, large picturesque Pathans, with evil-looking knives at their belts, shared the room with me. My uniform was no doubt a provocation to the young Congress Volunteers. They crowded against me and demanded, "Why did I want to see Gandhiji?" "Where," they demanded, "is Subhasji?" (Bose). One of them thrust a copper coin at me. "Did I see that?" I did. "Do you know that once our coins were made of gold, but the British took all the gold out of the country. That's why the Indians are poor." My comment that there was more to it than that was not well received.

From this embarrassment I was relieved by Pyeralal, a small and smooth man with a quiet voice. Unfortunately, Gandhiji was busy with the Khan, but if I returned the day after tomorrow Bapuji would see me. Meanwhile his prayer meeting was to start shortly, and if I cared to attend I should go round to the garden.

There was already a crowd sitting on the grass, smoking *bidris* and chewing betel nut, sellers of which moved among them. Most of the crowd was Hindu, but there were many Muslim women and some Parsees among them. There were also some Americans, who were in places of honour and busy with their cameras. The crowd was kept in order by teenage Congress Volunteers who manhandled some people, but not roughly. On a high platform were a bed and CBS and Indian radio microphones.

Presently Gandhi, with his entourage, emerged from the house, accompanied by his guru, Pyeralal and Abdul Gaffir Khan, a large ruddy-faced man, with close-cropped grey hair and beard, who could have been mistaken for an English farm worker. With him were his son and the chief of his Red Shirts. Gandhi himself looked younger and stronger than I had expected. When he appeared the crowd applauded. Gandhi and the Khan sat on the bed while prayers were chanted, first by Gandhi's guru in Hindi and then Muslim prayers in Urdu by Maulana Kalam Azad, the Muslim president of the Congress Party. Only once did the crowd join in the prayers, the rest of the time they talked and walked about. At the end a collection was taken for the *Harijans* (untouchables), while Gandhi, with the others, passed through the crowd while he said "Namaste" very sweetly. Two years later, at just such a meeting he was murdered.

When I presented my letter signed by Pyeralal at the gate two days later I spent half an hour talking to the young Congress Volunteers, who were much more friendly than at my previous visit. They told me about their military training, and said that of course they would join the army when they were free. Pyeralal came and spent ten minutes talking with me in the porch, sounding me about my political contacts.

Then we spent half an hour in discussion in the house. I asked him what should be done to alleviate the suffering of the Indian people. I received the conventional Congress/Gandhi answer: poverty was the result of British rule and particularly of the ruin of village industry: the best answer lay in Gandhi's revival of spinning and other village crafts, not in industrialisation (this was in Birla House!). He was wholly against the plan drawn up under the names of India's two largest capitalists, Tata and Birla (his host). But, I said, famine and epidemics made the matter urgent. He replied that relief merely scratched the surface. "The spinning wheel is the answer." What, I next asked, should the British do? "Recognise," he replied, "that you have no moral right to India. Make a declaration of Indian independence. Then, if you wished, you could help India, which would be only too ready to trade with you." Would the Hindu majority reach agreement with the minorities? He thought complete agreement would not be reached, but government would hurry to make a substantive agreement, but would allow "no cat and monkey" politics from third parties (the British) pulling chestnuts from the fire. Congress was pledged to abolish untouchability.

Would India be democratic? That was for Indians to work out: it could not be less democratic than it was at that moment. Then he turned the conversation on the power politics in Europe and the fate of Poland. I thought he was logical and consistent, but that the terrible events of the last five years had not influenced his outlook; that he would have given me the same answers in 1938 or earlier. We ended the discussion by his giving me an open invitation to stay at Gandhi's ashram at Sangirapatam. But I never had the chance.

Gandhi sitting as when I saw him, April 6th 1948.

Gandhi was keeping silence, giving answers in writing. He sat in a room draped with white sheets, spinning. My impression at the prayer meeting, that he was bigger than portrayed in cartoons, was correct. The flesh of his arms and legs was wrinkled by age and sun, but he was bigger physically, and had more flesh on his bones than I. For a man of 76 who had spent years in prison and had endured hunger strikes he was pretty good. There was an atmosphere of calm about him. What also struck me was that he seemed so ordinary: perhaps that was why he had such an influence.

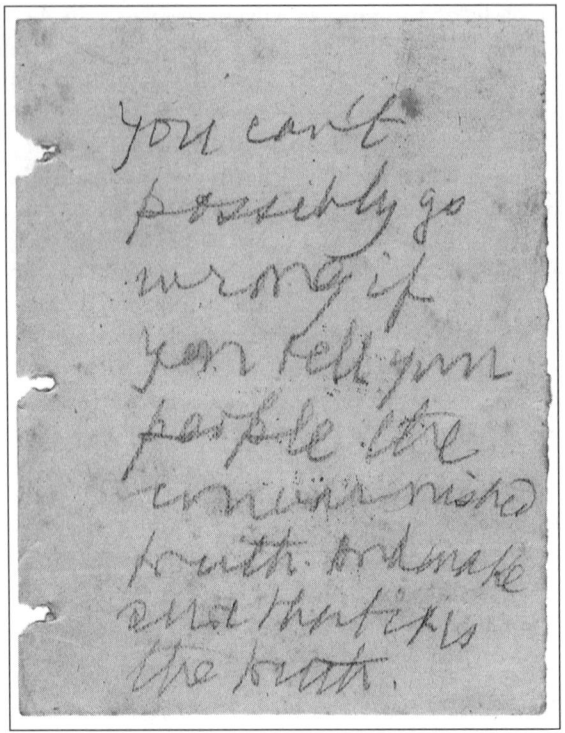

Gandhi's advice to me, April 6th 1945.

He bowed his head to me and indicated that I should come and sit by him. After a silence I paid my respects and asked what a friend of India should do to help. I had been distressed by much of that I had seen and wanted India to be independent. He took the stub of a pencil and wrote with it: "You cannot possibly go wrong if you tell your people the unvarnished truth, And make sure that it is the truth."

At this point my mind went blank. I could not think what to say or ask. All the possible questions I thought of later: "How would I know the truth?" (He would have said, I think, "Look in your heart") or about Hindus and Muslims, or Pakistan, would not come. It would be good to say that I had heard some political or spiritual truth. But I cannot; I dried up, and lost my opportunity. So I thanked him, wished him well, said "Nameste," and left.

Pyeralal said, "Come and have tea." We agreed that the British knew too little about India. He thought we should lose our standard of living if we gave up India. I disagreed and he finally agreed that the loss would be temporary. We talked of the two anti-Gandhi writers, Beverley Nichols and Katherine Mayo. He argued that the war would not strengthen democracy; India had no national defence and China had been left prostrate by the West. He agreed things might have been different in Europe, but added that there would be a worse war if the problems of Asia were not settled.

While we were talking, a little unshaven man in a dhoti and a striped shirt, with a collar-stud but no collar, came in. I was introduced to Birla, who asked me if I had come from Burma and what it was like there. The anomaly of one of India's richest men looking like a workman was striking, but not more so than the contradiction of talk about spinning wheels in the house of a great cotton manufacturer. But the greatest paradox was Gandhi sitting dressed and looking like a peasant in the centre of a palace. Nehru once said, "It costs a great deal of money to keep Gandhi in poverty."

As I was saying my thanks to Pyeralal, Abdul Gaffir Khan and his son came in to say goodbye. Outside the gate a newsman asked me to talk to him. I didn't.

The record of my discussions with Pyeralal may seem somewhat arcane, after half a century. But insofar as his views were those of Gandhi's entourage and were constantly pressed on the Old Man, they have some relevance to the tragedies which were to follow.

23 Echoes of Dickens

Kapila Khandrala was Secretary for Schools in Bombay City. She was a friend of Bill Carritt from their student days. Mohan introduced her to me as the person who could best tell me about Indian education. To me, Kapila seemed a very warm person and an impressive modern politician and educationalist – one of many outstanding Indian women at that time. She introduced me to S K Bhivandkar, Bombay Schools Superintendent, who was to be my guide round Bombay primary schools. He had, he told me, travelled in Europe and studied education in England, France, Switzerland and Italy – but remained a "good Indian".

A few days later, when we had made our visits, he invited me to lunch with his family, who were very welcoming, especially his wife. There were five children, a student son, who was not well and, I thought, a little spoiled, a lively attractive daughter of about 12, two little girls and a baby. Their home was furnished, in the English style, with diplomas and photos of relatives on the wall. In a glass cabinet he had a collection, of which he was very proud, of the little china ornaments that were sold in holiday centres, with the coat of arms and the name of the town. There were little jugs and pots, lighthouses and tortoises, inscribed Bournemouth, Blackpool, Margate, Skegness and so on. We ate various Indian dishes, with a prodigious amount of rice. The meal lasted all the afternoon, and over it I learned more about his opinions and feelings. He was very pro-British, but nationalist and liberal, pro-Congress and very hostile to the Muslim League;

pessimistic about India's economic future but convinced that a free India could help Britain.

When Kapila had introduced us, he sketched the organisation and problems of education in Bombay. Schooling was free and compulsory, making it the most progressive part of India. Primary schools were run by the Ministry of Schools Committee of which Kapila was the secretary. Secondary schools were run by the (Bombay) Provincial Government, Missionary and Aided Schools by Delhi. There wasn't much pre-primary schooling. Pupils could take matriculation, which had, until recently, been taken in English, but now with some subjects in their vernacular. The standard of matric was below that in England in Maths and English, otherwise it was the same.

In reply to my question he said that religion and caste were no problem in Bombay. Children accepted teachers of a different religion and untouchable children went to the same schools as the others, except for a few schools which took untouchables only. The real problem was lack of central government interest or finance. Bombay had to find at least 70% of the costs of its schools.

As a result, teachers were on the edge of starvation at a time of inflation. He himself had been head of a large secondary school on Rs. 150 (less than £9) a month – the top of the teachers' scale. Bombay City paid the primary teachers more than the Province paid the secondary teachers. But it was a pittance.

Our first visit together was to a Marathi-speaking slum school. Nothing in Dickens had prepared me. Forty children were sitting on benches in a dungeon-like room; some of them were outside in the passage used by the tenants in the rest of the building. A balcony gave an extension, but not in the monsoon. The sole teacher, who was young and looked depressed, had no teaching aids apart from a few colour prints and maps on the walls. The children were in rags, some in old coats. I looked at the lavatories and washhouse, which were shared with the tenants, and wished that I hadn't.

Our next visits were more cheerful: a large municipal welfare centre, six or seven different language primary schools for 1800 children. I met the heads who explained their problems; how in poor districts the parents were uneducated and gave no co-operation to the schools; how different languages made communication difficult; how the government and municipality did not take teachers into their confidence; how education was too academic and not sufficiently vocational; and how lack of literature in Marathi prevented teachers from knowing foreign methods.

But the school with a Telegu-speaking Tamil head over a multi-language intake had real achievements; attendance had improved, so had the children's health and sanitation – the clinical knowledge they were taught having spread to their parents. The school's own sanitation was excellent. In a mixed area communal tensions had been reduced by the school's influence. The children had a good physical education and play space but no field for football. The school had a debating society, Scout and Guide troops and schools visits.

We went on to two Urdu-speaking single-sex primary schools in a Muslim area. These also had good buildings with play spaces with seesaws and so on. On the walls were science charts and pictures of Tagore and Jinnah, and in the classrooms globes, models of animals and some scientific instruments. In the boys' school the head discussed discipline. He was a gentle man who did not believe in punishment. If boys were difficult it was because of home circumstances, and he tried to lead them along the right way by persuasion.

Our last visit of the day was to a training college for young Urdu-speaking Muslim women who were to become primary teachers. They took a 2-year diploma and then started teaching at Rs. 25 a month (£1 – £2). The principal came from a progressive Muslim family and was not in purdah. Her fifteen or so students were in purdah but were not wearing it while I visited because, I was told, not being a Muslim I did not rank as a man. So the young women could crowd round me with curiosity about a "non-man" soldier. The Principal was trying to bring them "out", so at the college and on picnics they did not wear purdah. They themselves would like to "come out" totally, but their parents said "no". There was, she said, hostile gossip about her and about the Schools Committee for appointing a woman who "didn't even look like a Muslim"! Perhaps this wasn't altogether surprising as she regarded herself as an Indian, spoke bitterly against Jinnah for making Muslims communal-conscious.

The students, she complained, had to be taught "from ABC" because their parents had kept them ignorant. Some girls came to the college with Mahrati as their mother tongue, but she had to teach them in Urdu. The common language of India should be English, but Gandhi insisted on it being Hindi. Her ideal was that of H G Wells' *Work, Wealth and Happiness of Mankind*. "Why should there be all these political parties? Why bring Stalin here and make him a god?"

She asked me to write in her visitors' book. I wrote that she was doing important and excellent work, which delighted her. In return she expressed herself pleased to meet a liberal-minded English person who wanted India to have more freedom – not at all like her idea of the military.

Over tea and cakes Kapila said that about a quarter of the Bombay primary schools, with one in ten of the children, were like the slum school I saw. Her main aim – with very limited resources – was to improve buildings and equipment within the existing framework. She agreed that religious and language barriers did prejudice teacher training in the backward state, for example, of history knowledge and materials, so she was hiring a programme of films to show teachers. On the other hand untouchability was not a problem in schools, as it was in social life. Muslims, she said, had the lowest educational standards, but the Muslim League had helped to raise them and improve school attendance.

24 Schooling on Communal Lines?

A few days later I was met by a Hindu woman schools inspector who was to take me to some secondary schools at Kapila's request. She told me that, twenty years earlier, she had been one of the earliest to flout convention and to fight her parents for her right to education, and that, while there had been some change of attitude, there was still immensely deep-rooted prejudice against women earning and so "neglecting their homes". Nursing was more tolerated than teaching even though nurses could devote even less time to their homes.

The standard of the two schools, both for boys, to which she took me was high, as far as it was possible to judge. The first was the Aryan Education Society's Boys' High School (for Hindus "Aryan" means something different from Hitler's racism). It comprised a primary and a small pre-primary as well as a secondary school. In all there were some 1700 pupils. The twenty or so pre-primary boys were taught by the Montessori method, one group doing action songs, the other drawing their own ideas. The mistress told me that in 1942 they all drew planes and war images but that now they had forgotten the war. They certainly seemed very happy and well cared for.

The primary school was horribly overcrowded, housing another school while the army had taken over its building. The secondary school was more fortunate, with an excellent library donated by a Hindu benefactor, an Indian gymnasium, a kitchen, tuck shop, and reasonably-equipped laboratories with an enthusiastic master teaching in English (other subjects were in Marathi).

I took tea and sweetmeats with the headmaster and the assistant head, who had shown me round. They told me how discipline was maintained by class pupils, elected each year by the boys, and that the two "Aryan Troops" (equivalent to scouts) with their elected leader had to prevent mishaps during school breaks. There was a "parliament" with annual elections and campaigns to choose one representative from each class. Religious studies concentrated on getting rid of caste and sectarianism. The pupils also helped in the literacy drive, either with propaganda or taking classes. Each evening some fifty boys from poorer homes came to the school to study. As elsewhere, their two main problems were the poor pay of teachers and lack of co-operation from parents. When 700 parents were invited to the school only 70 came; now they were trying class parents' days.

The secondary schools I had seen seemed well equipped, though each was for a separate religious community, and I could not judge the standard of teaching. My visit to St. Xavier's High School presented no such question, for the reputation of Jesuit education in Asia was high. The school had sixty teachers (fifteen of them Jesuit fathers) for about 1100 pupils. The building was imposing, somewhat churchlike and splendidly equipped. The hall had cinema equipment, stage, dressing rooms, large costume and make-up facilities; there were first rate laboratories; geography rooms with projectors and working models, corridors filled with biology specimens; charts showing food values and dietary advice with Indian seeds and plants on show. My guide told of the school debating society and scout troop. Discipline, he said, was kept by prefects appointed by the head. There was no corporal punishment. The pupils were middle class, paying Rs. 5 - 8 a month (16 Rs. = £1). The school received a small government grant. Most of the staff, but only a few of the pupils, were Christian. None, however, was spared Catholic propaganda. In the comfortable clubrooms for older pupils Catholic literature was on sale, *Catholic Herald* pamphlets attacking birth control and "atheistic Communism" were laid out. They did not attack the Russian people, only Stalin and the Communist government. Around the hall was a large date chart of world history. In 1936, it recorded, took place the Spanish Civil War: "Freedom v. Bolshevism"! Most of the Fathers were German or Irish and I had been warned that there was sympathy with the German cause in the school.

My last visit was with a very gracious Parsee, Mrs Dalas, a schools superintendent, who took me to the large Parsee school, pre-primary and primary schools mixed, secondary girls only. I found myself promoted – I was introduced as Professor Fyrth and given a big bunch of flowers. I was shown the kitchens which prepared midday meals for the under-fives and for 550 of the poorer children in the schools, as well as breakfasts for the very poor; the kitchens were very clean and well appointed. The school put great store by health and hygiene and, I was told, children who were rickety when they first came became healthy. A woman doctor attended the school part-time.

The schools were as well equipped as St Xavier's (Parsees and Jesuits were the richest communities), but the Parsee school in the suburb of Dadar was in pleasanter surroundings, with its own gardens, where gardening was taught. It also had its own seaside holiday camp, eighty miles away. In August 1942, 450 children had been evacuated there. The school library was very good. I was told that Dickens and Mrs Henry Wood were the most popular authors.

Again and again I had heard that parents were indifferent to their children's education, and Kapila told me that often they did not know the names of their child's teachers. She thought some of the answer was in adult education. I knew of the literacy campaign launched in 1936-37 jointly by Congress Party and the Communist Party. I knew, too, of classes held at midnight so that women could come after their day's domestic work was finished!

A meeting to which Kapila took me was a disappointment. Some 250 teachers had turned up, presumably hoping for some plan or scheme for adult education. What they got was a speech of airy generalisation. When I started work in adult education after the war, I was to hear so much of the same.

25 Waiting for a Renaissance

An exhibition of paintings by the "Bengal Group" was disappointing. (We had gone because the Bob Hope film was booked up.) The lighting was poor – in one room non-existent, as the bulbs had not been replaced. Homeless families were living in the corridors. Apart from three excellent famine studies, the paintings were either traditional Hindu religious studies, or imitations of Moghul art or Impressionist paintings of Indian landscapes.

Some days later, Chittaprosad, the left-wing artist whose black and white line drawings in *People's War* I had admired, talked to me about the sorry state of Indian art and architecture. In Moghul times and earlier, there were great artists and architects employed by the emperors, and these were also engaged in folk art. Persian architecture was imported, but became absorbed into Indian traditions. By contrast, the British, when they overthrew the Moghuls, imported their own architecture without adaptation, so wealthy Indians copied these. Handicrafts were crushed by British machine imports and artists starved, while Indian arts decayed. Folk art forms had remained static for 150 years. Nor had there been any musical development. There were ancient forms at one end and "bazaar" and film music at the other.

Earlier in the century the Bengal "renaissance", under the influence of Tagore, had rejected everything European but did not understand the Indian folk forms which it tried to revive.[11] Now a feeling of frustration permeated intellectuals. The Bengal Group of artists was progressive in that they had formed a group to work together and were interested in and critical of society, but not really in touch with it.

Chittaprosad explained that the reasons why Westerners found it hard to understand Indian art lay in the vast difference in form between Indian and Western art, springing from wide colour differences in the richness of life and vegetation and its influence.

At the Tagore school at Santiniketan he had studied folk art and tried to understand the reasons for and meanings of it. He belonged to no movement, but at his home in Chittagong the political movement was all around him at the time of the armoury raid. He studied European art but did not copy it, though he greatly admired Picasso. He had tried to explain scientific theories to the people through folk forms but failed. It had seemed to him that art was useless. But the Japanese invasion and the famine had made him try again to show people the richness of life. Then he was surprised to discover how, against all previous theories, common people appreciated and criticised his art.

He asked me to see and criticise his current work, a colour sketch for a larger canvas to be called *The Tragedy of Bengal*. I protested that I was in no way qualified to judge – but he wanted my opinion in the way the he wanted the opinions of ordinary, untrained Indian people. The work was clearly based on the ideas of Picasso's *Guernica*, adapted to Bengal folk forms. It was powerful and moving. The folk arts and the learning of Bengal contrasted with the horror of the present: ruined farms, famine-wracked bodies, Japanese bombs, vice and prostitution, the mother country consumed by nameless horrors, the skeleton arms of bureaucracy grasping the motherland and protecting chaos, the patriots naked and unable even to look at the scene. Colour contrasts, violet and grey, red and yellow, orange and green, heightening the horror – perhaps he did not know how much of the painters of the Northern Renaissance, Cranach and Breughel, were in it.

After independence, Indian traditional music and dance began to be appreciated in the West. Indian films were shown at art cinemas. By the 1970s a generation of younger writers was producing novels which experimented with Western techniques to express contemporary Indian themes. But two centuries in a cultural cul-de-sac are not easy to slough off.

26 Seeds of Hope

Signs of a cultural revival were to be seen, in 1945, either in those areas which had little or no link with the India of pre-British days, such as science and economics, or where artists or writers wished to use their art to appeal to the people in a way that would help to achieve a new and more creative India.

The most popular of the arts – the cinema – showed the contradictions of the time. Second in size only to Hollywood, the Indian film industry attracted millions of cinema goers each week, but most of the films were purely using the technology of the West to provide escapism for the masses, who, goodness knows, needed an escape from their everyday lives. There were four types of film: musicals, sentimental love stories, historical epics, depicting the glories of the past, and occasionally something more serious with a lesson for today. No comment on modern India was possible, the censorship was rigid, but the audience might draw conclusions.

The three Indian films which I saw followed this pattern. *Shakletala* was a musical set in the first century BC. The colour was crude, the love story sentimental and the animals could have been created by Walt Disney. But there was some very pleasant singing and dancing and the film portrayed an unexpected spirit of independent womanhood. The audience loved it. *Samraj Chandragupta* was an historical spectacle of Alexander the Great invading India and being defeated – the Macedonian soldiers carried Roman eagles with the SPQR sign! There were spectacular battle scenes – and a naval battle straight from Ben Hur and a cast of thousands. It was poor technically, though broadly patriotic.

The best was *Ram Shastri*, a moral/patriotic story with fine photography and beautiful acting. It told the story of a famous chief justice of the 16th-17th century; devoted from childhood to truth, learning and justice, who fought against injustice and class justice in high places. The message was that in "the old days" justice and honesty were respected. Films could make no application of the moral to the present, but the audience would understand. It was from the makers of such films that, after independence, the new Indian cinema, produced by Satajit Ray, was to come.

Another example of something new and lively was the Indian People's Theatre, which presented drama in Calcutta and ballet and puppet theatre in Bombay and other cities. It took folk art and old religious forms and gave them a new content and meaning, showing the oppression of the Indian people and their struggles against famine and hoarders. It was unashamedly agit-prop, but it was alive and very popular.

But my most exciting cultural experience in Bombay was a "conference" (a public poetry reading) of Hindi-speaking Muslim poets, held under the stars and floodlights on the central Maidan. I sat on the ground with several thousand spectators. I was not in uniform and the man next to me looked at my lighter skin and asked, "Are you from the frontier?" My answer roused interest around and he offered to translate or tell me the gist of poems. The poets sat garlanded on a dais with microphones. Most of them intoned, in the traditional way, their old and overworked themes of love and despair. One old religious poet and some revolutionary ones recited their works and those the audience seemed to prefer. Powerful religious poems and progressive ones – one attacked the hypocrisy of certain religious men – and particularly good stanzas were welcomed with cries of "Ah-ha", "Oh-he", and "Shabash" (bravo) from the audience.

My one visit to a scientific centre was to the Hafkine Institute, the foremost in India for preparing serums, vaccines and antibiotics. Dr Hubbin, the Director, showed me the whole process, preparation of organisms, injection into animals, testing and so on. He showed me plasma and penicillin preparation. I remember most the preparation of anti-snakebite serum; the milking of the poison from cobras, Russell's vipers, krates and the deadly little frosias. They were made to bite into containers and the venom was injected into some splendid horses to produce antibodies. Stroking the snakes, I found them neither scaly nor slimy – just smooth and muscular. Dr Hubbin told me that at first – as in the 1900 plague epidemic – there was great prejudice against vaccines and injections. But the prejudice was being broken down, although there was need for education, and propaganda squads should go to villages. Asked about ayurvedic medicine, he replied that there had been practically no research. Some herbs and drugs might be useful, but research was needed. There was a lot of quackery. In the villages people were poor and ignorant. There were no doctors or drugs, "So what is there for them but to turn to the gods?" The next day I returned to Ahmednagar.

27 Kelkhar

He suggested that we should meet by the small temple in a grove of trees, just outside one of the city gateways of Ahmednagar and not far from the fort.

I knew from reading *British Soldier in India* that Kelkhar, an artist, had been a good friend of Clive Branson, and that he had welcomed Clive into his home many times. Clive's drawings of Usha, Kelkhar's wife, their children and family were reproduced in the book.

Kelkhar the artist, Ahmednagar (sketch by Clive Branson)

A small temple among the trees sounded romantic. It wasn't. The temple, little more than a shrine, was undecorated, its darkness lit by only a feeble little light, which barely showed the crude representation of the god. All round the temple were little piles of dried, and not so dried, human ordure: no doubt the offerings of the devotees, or perhaps just of passers-by who found the shelter of the trees convenient. The trees were few and stunted, surrounded by the dusty plain. Immediately outside the entrance to the city was a municipal rubbish tip.

I sat on a log near the trees, and Kelkhar came, a small man, smiling and friendly. We sat and talked for an hour, the first of many such meetings. I cannot recall what we talked about, but in a letter to my sister Paddy I wrote:

> I have made the friendship of Clive Branson's artist friend [a circumlocution for the censor] ... We've had several interesting talks together about the country, [meaning the politics of the country] about art and about Clive. I think he considers Clive was the greatest man who ever lived.

He also told me about his family. One evening he excused himself that he could not stay long because it was "the time of the month" for his dear wife, and he must go and prepare the family meal. I thought what a good husband he was, assuming that perhaps she was not feeling well. Only later did I learn that Hindus believe that at such a time a woman is unclean.

Once, when we were talking, a bullock cart came out of the city loaded with mangoes. Behind followed a trail of ragged women and children with tins and baskets. The mangoes were tipped onto the rubbish heap and, immediately, the women and children threw themselves onto them, carrying them off. Kelkhar explained that the mangoes were being dumped because they were infected with cholera. Rather innocently, I asked, "Shouldn't we do something to stop them?" He shrugged and said, "Those people are very hungry. They will die of starvation, anyway."

Shortly before we left Ahmednagar, he said that his "dear wife" would like me to come for a meal and meet the family. Notices had been posted putting the city out of bounds to troops because of plague. I did not wish to be picked up out of bounds by the redcaps. Kelkhar said there was no plague in the city and was clearly disappointed. Later, I wished that I had risked it. But he had recently told me that I must be very careful and look out for myself.

To keep the charging engines, large and small, running, thirty-gallon drums of petrol were regularly delivered to my workshop. But they had been containing only 20-25 gallons. I checked with Reg in the transport lines and he said their drums were also short. So I reported to the CO and the drums came with their full quota. I told Kelkhar this story, as an item of news. He said he knew, though he did not know my part in the matter. Nothing was secret in an Indian town. He told me that the Indian contractor, who supplied the petrol, was well known to be making his fortune at the army's expense. The English Service Corps Major, who was responsible for allocating contracts, also had a share in the business, out of which he had had built a luxurious new bungalow. The two responsible were very angry at what had happened, so I should take care. It was a strong reason for not risking a visit to the city.

Not long before the squadron left Ahmednagar, Kelkhar said that his headmaster, an American, would like me to come to the school and talk to senior pupils about English education. The school was outside the city. The head introduced me to some twenty 16-17 year old boys, and left Kelkhar to chair the meeting. I talked about the different kinds of schools, public schools, secondary and primary, which were very much based on our class structure, and outlined the new (Butler) Education Act which was going to make secondary education available for all. It was probably, for them, a very dull talk. Kelkhar asked for questions. There was some shuffling and giggling and looking at one boy, who rose and asked: "Are there any good Englishmen?" After my rather fumbling affirmation that of course there were, he asked, "Then why do we never see them?" For me it was a chastening experience, for the boys – no doubt – a little triumph, but for poor Kelkhar it was an embarrassment.

28 VE Day: Ancient Glories

From April to June the land baked and crumbled. Little dust demons danced across it and collapsed. Mynah birds, robins and an occasional crow, came gasping to the dripping tap on the parade ground. The fort gave us a little shelter from the sun and we lay on our charpoys in the afternoon, sleeping or reading. Some men would tease the pretty little Muslim boy who ran around with mugs of tea. "*Chockra, Chockra,*" they called, "*Char Manta.*" He would shout furiously, "*Chockra Nai, hum Chockri.*" (I'm not a little girl, I'm a little boy) and bare his evidence at his tormentors.

Taffy, the Liverpool policeman, went into hospital with tapeworms. Lievesley and I borrowed a jeep and went to visit him. On the way we saw a huge, black swirling demon rushing towards us. We leapt from the jeep, ran, with grit stinging our faces, to some empty huts, where we slammed and bolted the doors and shutters as the violent dust storm hit the buildings.

At the end of the first week in May Germany surrendered. The CO said we must light a bonfire on a nearby hill to let all the villages around know that the war in Europe was over. The villagers would have cared little for far away events, but we were glad of a celebration, so that evening we lit and stood around the bonfire and argued with the CO, who still thought that the Munich Agreement had been a good thing. The Foreman said we should have listened to Nehru, and I, having drunk two foul rums, added that I considered Chamberlain a villain. The Foreman added that after the war Britain would be a socialist country and others – especially the Welsh – joined in his support.

We were given a holiday. Led by the Foreman and the Captain, we piled into jeeps and trucks to visit the Alora Caves, one of the wonders of India. There were some thirty "caves", Buddhist, Hindu and Jain, dating from about 600-1000 AD, not built but carved from the top down out of the hill. The engineering feat alone was a wonder, even more so the sculptures and carvings made not from blocks of stone, but also hewn from the native rock. The craftsmen/artists who made them could not have afforded a single mistake. The Buddhist caves, originally part of a monastery, were plain caverns with the Buddha as the only statue. The Jain caves were also little ornamented. The greatest wonder lay in the Hindu caves with their statues and carvings.

Most impressive was the great Kaihasa cave, twice the size of the Parthenon, to excavate which 200,000 tons of rock had had to be removed. In the centre was a large Shivaling, the Hindu phallic fertility symbol. A poor middle-aged woman was rubbing her lower parts against it, presumably in the hope that she would bear. Among the carvings was one of a long dead queen, that was both beautiful and erotic; but most striking of all was a sculpture of what we were told were the equivalent in Hindu mythology of the "Fates": three old famine women, almost naked, with skeleton ribs and haggard jaws, carved long before the European Renaissance, and, for me, more moving than any classical sculpture.

After we had eaten our picnic, we drove to the 14th century city of Dulatabad, intended as the capital of India by the Moghul Sultan of Delhi. Now it was deserted. Picture a walled city the size of the City of London, with minarets, temples, buildings that had once been both temples and mosques, shared by Hindus and Moslems; with large tanks for ritual bathing, streets of shops and streets of houses, with the lizards and birds its only dwellers, apart from a couple of watchmen. In the centre was the high Citadel which we approached through an underground passage before climbing the steep steps to the top. Halfway up were iron doors which could be slid across and, with fires lit on them, would become a red hot impassable barrier. At the very top was a massive cannon cast in bronze. Standing by it we could see to where, beyond the city walls, farmers were ploughing their fields with oxen, as they would have done when the city was alive. I thought of Shelley's poem *Ozymandias*, and of Omar Khayyam:

They say the lion and the lizard keep
the courts where Jamshyd gloried and drank deep.

In the evening we went into the modern city of Aurangabad for a celebratory dinner at a hotel – the only one I entered in India. It had that rare thing in India, a WC with a pedestal seat. We all went several times, just for the pleasure of working the flush.

29 VL Night: Present Triumphs

With June came the rain. There was not much in the first five days, but by mid-June the rain was falling pleasantly, we were cooler, and the world had a green film.

With the rain came news that there was to be a general election – on 5 July. Political discussion waxed. We listened to radio speeches and were paraded each day to hear the big guns of Labour, Liberal and Conservative booming – no Communists or Commonwealth voices. Churchill was voted a failure, even our Conservatives thought he had done himself harm with his ridiculous talk of a Labour "Gestapo".

Most of the unit considered itself to be Labour, though many of them had not registered or would not be voting. This was so throughout the forces – had all voted, the Labour victory would have been even greater. I had nominated Harry Welford as my proxy, unaware that he would be stricken with TB. On 5 July he went from his bed to cast his vote and mine, before being taken to the sanatorium.

We had only three Conservatives, of very different types. Johnnie Dance, Walls, and our vicious racist. Ginger, my tent mate in the Arakan, tended to mirror the views of the two former as he had previously mirrored mine – but he was not voting.

There was also much apathy, especially among those like Bill the cook, who had white-collar jobs before the war and who had been in India so long they were disillusioned with everything political and all in authority. These were completely fed up with the Tories, but felt out of their element with Labour.

At this time I was friendly with two Labour Party members from one of our battalions who visited me regularly to borrow my newspaper, and together we walked on the walls of the fort, discussing the latest news. For a short time before the election was announced the *Daily Worker* had been in favour of a coalition government of those who had played a part in victory. This was happening in France and Italy, and fitted in with the Yalta agreement. It was a foolish policy and they let me know it. Fortunately it was abandoned almost as soon as we heard about it, and before the campaign began.

On voting day a mock election was held in their regiment and these two arranged that I was invited to stand as the Communist candidate. I wrote to my sister Paddy about the evening:

> About 120 people turned up all very keen, including the Colonel who made a very good contribution ... The Tory and Liberal candidates opened up and were fairly flat ... and the Conservative was somewhat heckled. After (an) interval for refreshments came the "thunder on the left". For the first time in two years I was able to make such a speech and really went to town. The audience rose to the points with roars and cheers.

I recall attacking the poverty of health and education for the majority, unemployment and the appeasement of Hitler.

The Labour candidate made a good fighting speech and they gave him a terrific reception. Then came questions and attacks from the floor and that was the most exciting and invigorating part of the evening with good cut and thrust exchanges. Finally (at 11.30) the ballot result: Labour 58, Communist 21, Tory 14, Liberal 9. It's ages since I've enjoyed an evening so much.

When the election results were announced on 26 July we all gathered round the radios. As the results came in the Labour people became more elated, the Tories more bewildered. The second, decisive, batch came through in the evening. With each Labour gain the cheers grew louder, and when John Grigg, Minister for the Army, and Leo Amery, Secretary of State for India, lost their seats the cheers must have been heard beyond the walls of the fort. The racist Tory sat obscenely abusing the Labour Party and trade unions and repeating "The country will have to pay for this." Walls was fulminating "Another five years of being ordered about" and "We'll have to fill a form in triplicate when we want toilet paper." Johnnie Dance was consoling himself, "I've been a trade unionist for years and glad of it." In the days that followed people talked about "our government" and were saying, "we will have to help them now instead of criticising."

A few days later I was invited back to the regiment which had held the mock election to give a talk on my pre-war visit to the Soviet Union. About eighty people, of all ranks, came to hear me. I do not remember what I said. No doubt I told them what I had seen. No doubt it was a rosy picture – such as we then used to give. No doubt it included nothing about the black side of the picture or Stalin's many crimes and brutality, which were then unknown to me. Whatever I did say, it was well received, there were many questions but no hostility. At that time it was not only those of the left who thought well of the Soviets, and no doubt both I and my audience projected onto our picture of the Soviet Union many features which we would have liked to see in our own country. We also knew how much the victory in Europe owed to the Red Army.

30 VJ Day: Preparations for the Future

We were told that we had been brought to the fort to prepare for Operation Zipper. This was to be the sea-borne invasion of Malaya. Our tanks were to storm the Morib Beaches in the Straits of Malacca and crush the Japanese. Our Signals Unit had no rehearsal for this deadly operation.

We were simply told that when we drove our vehicle from the landing craft into the sea we must keep our foot hard on the accelerator, for if we stalled water would run up the exhaust pipe and we should be stuck in the sea. For the rest, we waterproofed our vehicles, engines and batteries.

When the last battery terminal, the last sparking plug and the last radio had been waterproofed with a sort of plasticine, the General-in-Command Southern Signals arrived to inspect us. The Tailor's Dummy brought him to my workshop and introduced me; "I want you to meet L/Cpl Fyrth, Sir; he's a member of the Communist Party." "How interesting," said the General, "You go ahead, Major, I'd like to have a chat with L/Cpl Fyrth." So the General and the L/Cpl sat down together and, for ten minutes or so, discussed post-war policies. At that time the Establishment clearly thought that the left would be an important force after the war. One question he asked was my attitude to conscription, and seemed satisfied when I explained that in general I preferred a conscript army to a professional one, as being nearer to the people.

Then, first one and then a second atom bomb were dropped. At that time we were all completely ignorant of what that meant. So were all the members of Attlee's cabinet and, probably, Truman's administration. Neither we nor they knew anything of the radiation resulting, the health risks or the consequences for world politics. American and British politicians blithely talked about "a powerful bomb which harnessed the forces of nature", without the least idea what that meant. All we knew was that, ten days later, the Japanese surrendered, and we were glad. We would live through Operation Zipper.

On morning parade, the Tailor's Dummy addressed us: "Well, men, you've heard the news. I'm afraid it means that we've been done out of our show. But there may be Jap units which haven't heard the news. They may resist ... they may resist. There may still be medals to be won." Mutterings of "silly bugger", "stupid idiot", or more obscene words, ran back and forth along our lines. Our Indian colleagues, standing behind us, remained impassive.

31 Zipper Comes Unzipped

We left the fort while it was still dark; Iqubal, a young Punjabi, who shared the jeep with me, looked back at the long line of headlamps and said, "It's like Diwali." He was a gentle young man, popular with his colleagues. As we chatted it became clear that he was not enchanted by army life. I asked him why he had joined; he told me that, when he was in his last year at school, a visiting official told the students that if they wished to pass their matric they should volunteer for the army. They did.

That night we spent in Deolali, then the main army centre in western India; a vast and depressing area of army huts and buildings, set in a flat, featureless landscape, said to be unbearably hot and dusty in summer, muddy and miserable in the monsoon. For very many soldiers this was India – the only civilians they met were *char wallahs*, *dhobi wallahs* and the like. No wonder most British ORs hated India.

We were crowded into huts with young paratroopers, eighteen to twenty year olds, being flown out from Germany and the Rhine crossing to the Far East. To us they seemed schoolboys, sitting reading their comics.

The following nights were pleasanter, as we camped on the dockside in Bombay. The first night we were told not to leave the docks. But a group of us hid in a truck carrying old tyres, and so passed through the gates. I went to see Mohan and the others at the Raj Bhavan.

The next day we were allowed out and our group enjoyed the pleasure of fresh iced lemon at an Iranian cafe. The Brigadier's cockney driver, an East Ender whose stories gave us many laughs, tried to persuade us that if we went into the cafe we would contract some dreadful stomach complaint, and stood on the other side of the road nervously waiting for us to collapse. One evening we saw Laurence Olivier's *Henry the Fifth*.

We loaded onto an old Indian tramp steamer, SS Floristan, and wallowed sickeningly through the late monsoon seas towards Malaya. One poor young man started being seasick while watching the ship rise and fall by the dockside. I went round with a tin tied round my neck for the bad moments. When we reached the quiet waters of the Malacca Straits we heard that Operation Zipper had come unzipped. Military Intelligence did not know that the Morib Beaches by Port Swettenham, which had been chosen for the landings, contained quicksands. The first wave of armoured vehicles to go ashore had stuck deep. It would take days to dig them out and find alternative beaches. (Aldous Huxley had said that under "intelligence" the *Encyclopedia Britannica* gives "Intelligence Human", "Intelligence Animal", "Intelligence Military"!) No accounts of the war seemed to mention this farce that could have been a tragedy, until I read the last volume of Paul Scott's *Raj Quartet – A Division of the Spoils*. Scott had been on Operation Zipper, and recorded how British commanders had lined up defeated Japanese commanders to show what they could have been up against: orders are given for the landing and men and vehicles left the landing craft and begun to advance. "After going fifty yards though, something odd happens. The leaders of the files of soldiers in the centre suddenly disappeared beneath the bland scarcely rippling surface and on one of the flanks the line of vehicles sank equally suddenly, not completely like the men but up to their superstructures."

SS Floristan was ordered to wait. So for days we moved slowly up and down the straits, watching the flying fishes and an occasional shark fin and waiting. We had run out of food. The Army Service Corps had, with economical care, given us just enough to last the planned ten days of the voyage. But we still had ships biscuits, herrings in tomato sauce, California yellow cling peaches and apricot jam. Breakfast was ship's biscuits and jam, our main meal biscuits and herrings in tomato sauce, our final food of the day biscuits and yellow cling peaches.

Ship's biscuits, which caused naval mutinies in the 18th century, are almost inedible, teeth can scarcely dent them, water – even boiling water – will not soften them. Tinned peaches were enjoyed at many Sunday teas before the war – but not when you have to eat them every day. I can still taste the metallic tang of the tinned herrings which I vowed would never again pass my lips.

Luckily, my relations with our Indian troops, who had enough food, could earn me a curry with chapattis. At that time most British soldiers would rather have gone foodless than eaten "wog food".

We grew hungry and discontented. Our Captain, who was as hungry as we were, declared that this was an emergency and opened the American "Pacific rations", issued for jungle warfare: tinned meat, concentrated fruit bars and other delights.

Soon afterwards we climbed down rope ladders onto landing craft and drove our jeeps and trucks through the sea to the beaches near Port Dickson.

32 A Small Paradise

We lived, for a fortnight, a Robinson Crusoe life, housed, together with large spiders, in Japanese coolie huts, swimming two or three times a day in the warm sea – hoping there were no sharks or jellyfish about. We lazed under the palm trees and sat in the cafes by the tiny harbour or Port Dickson, with its two streets of Chinese shops, two or three warehouses and a stone jetty. We drank coffee, served with fresh pineapple, watched the brightly coloured fishing boats and became used to the all-pervading smell of dried fish.

Because we were on the equator darkness came soon after six o'clock and our hut had no light but an old hurricane lamp. A few of us would walk a little after dark and one evening, seeing a light in a small house, we knocked, went in and sat down in a bare wooden room where we held a long conversation which neither side understood, with two old Chinese men and a boy. The house was scrubbed clean, although it had no furniture except two wooden chairs for the old men. We gave them some cigarettes and they gave us a pile of worthless Japanese Malayan dollars.

The Japanese did not loot the country, they paid for what they had. Every officer of the rank of Colonel upwards was given a press to print the money, which soon became worthless. The British made a huge bonfire in Kuala Lumpur and burned all the paper dollars they could find. The standard currency became a tin of 50 cigarettes; not to be smoked but used as coinage.

The children from next door came to see us and laughed when we showed them a cartoon of one of our squadron. So we went back to camp and collected sweets and chocolate, lemonade crystals, matches and biscuits and distributed them. Their family gave us two pineapples, but they were unripe and had a bad effect on those who ate them.

Other peasant houses showed the same bare poverty, but with none of the squalor of an Indian village and the poor, unlike the Indian poor, did not seem to be completely demoralised.

I am glad to have seen Malaya (as we called it then) while it was still, believably, the land of Conrad and Maugham; before its beaches were given over to tourist hotels, its roads and fields buried under motorways and "cybercities", its mountains and jungles scarred by huge quarries and doubtful dam projects, and its towns dominated by the towers of international finance.

Romanticism of course. No doubt there are fewer bare wooden peasant huts, perhaps fewer slum dwellers in Singapore. Certainly the middle class will have every comfort and convenience they wish. But the main beneficiaries have been a small number of very rich people in the peninsula and in the financial centres of the world, whose wealth is beyond the dreams of Aladdin. And is so much destruction necessary?

33 A Night at the Chinese Opera

Kuala Lumpur (KL) was then a sprawling city and, like other towns in the peninsula, largely Chinese. Its inner alleyways were forbidden to us, especially at Chinese festivals such as the Chinese national day, "The Tenth of the

Tenth" (10 October), commemorating the overthrow of the Manchu Emperors in 1911.

We lived in what had been houses of the wealthy. There were rooms around a formal garden, which was tended by Japanese prisoners, tall, large-boned men from the north. At first our quarters were cleaned by young Chinese women, but these quickly withdrew when one of the squadron made a pass.

I had a large workshop for my engines, shared with some oversized crawling creatures. An eight-inch centipede which I killed and threw out was immediately seized by black ants who lifted it to carry up to their entrance hole in the wall. But it was too heavy for them. A few inches up the wall they dropped it, picked it up again and dropped it again and again ... and again. When I came out during the night to check the engines, they were still trying and still failing. So I cut the centipede into segments. Within thirty seconds every bit had disappeared into their tunnel.

The days were hot and sticky until the late afternoon, when the wind changed, bringing rain off the sea at the same time each day. The Tailor's Dummy having disappeared, we had a new CO, a large, friendly man who decreed that, during daylight, we should wear nothing but our underpants while in camp. In the evenings he often invited a few of us at a time to come and have a drink and a chat with him. He asked me, "Why aren't you an officer?" On being told that I'd given the wrong answer when asked, "Do you play rugger?", he laughed and said he had been asked, "Do you ride?" and that when he replied, "Not horses!", it had been decided that he was officer material.

One memory of Kuala Lumpur is of a football match against the Jesuit brothers at their monastery. The German brother who was marking me at outside left spent more time warning me, in hushed tones, against the Communists, than he did in ensuring that I did not get past him with the ball. After the game we were shown round their hospital, where starving children taken from the streets were being nursed. They lay with wizened limbs, distended stomachs and wide, apathetic eyes. Everywhere there were such victims in the wake of the war. It seemed a mockery to sit down to tea afterwards.

Two events stand out, the Chinese opera and the Chinese music hall, both held in the open-air theatre of the amusement park. The Chinese opera was very unlike *Cosi Fan Tutti*. It had an orchestra, singers in costumes, and told a story; there any similarity ended. Fortunately, the story was a traditional legend, known to the audience, because the words could not be heard. The moment the singers opened their mouths the instruments broke into such a torrent of sound – discordant to western ears – that arias were drowned. The same outbursts accompanied spoken words. The costumes were magnificent and the movements and gestures of the players went a long way to explaining the narrative. For a moment I was taken back to Shakespeare's theatre, when chairs were placed on the side of the stage and older and clearly more important members of the audience sat on them. It was a fascinating spectacle – but the first hour was enough: the opera would have gone on for many more.

The music hall was more accessible but poor stuff. There was a comedian dressed as, and trying to imitate, Charlie Chaplin, and there were two Chinese teenage girls singing popular songs; the (Malayan) "Taram Boulam" (Bright Moonlight) and (Chinese) a song which sounded like "Meekway an Meekway" which was heard everywhere. Both were later played by British dance bands, one as "Malayan Moon" and the other something about "Come on back to old Malaya." Neither took on. Other acts were jugglers, acrobats and such.

At one of these events, two small Chinese boys – probably of six or seven years – sitting in front of me kept turning round, whispering and giggling. By and by, one of them knelt on his chair, reached over slowly and gingerly and gently stroked my nose; both of them collapsed in laughter. The Chinese see Europeans as people with big noses, red faces and angry eyes.

34 A Storm Drawing Near

There was in Malaya, besides the Chinese who dominated the towns, the beautiful and easy-going Malays who were mostly countryfolk, and the Indians who had been brought in by the British as labourers, a substantial Eurasian population, descendants of Portuguese, Dutch or British fathers and Malay or Chinese mothers. Unlike the Eurasians in India, they happily thought of themselves as Asians.

Three Eurasians had been recruited to work in our office at Kuala Lumpur, a man and two women. They were middle-class Roman Catholics, very interested in the British royal family, of whom they were pleased to be subjects, and they were conservative in politics.

They were immensely hospitable, inviting me, Johnnie Dance and Lievesley to have dinner with them one Saturday and then to spend Sunday with them. We were given all sorts of delicious dishes – the source of which at a time of shortage we did not enquire. On Sunday they hired a terrible old four-seater banger into which we three and six of their family squeezed; and like many other such parties in ancient cars, left over from the occupation, went sightseeing. They took us to the sea at Port Swettenham, where the Brigade would have landed but for the quicksands. It was a small river port, which held three or four ships, a little larger than Port Dickson. On the way back we visited the palace of the Sultan of Selingor, the feudal Malay aristocrat who had ruled the largest state in Malaya. He was currently under arrest for having danced at the end of the Japanese string, after many years at the end of the British.

Our two evenings with them were very enjoyable except for a brother-in-law who became unpleasantly drunk. They told us about the occupation and it was fascinating to see how closely in families ran the threads of resistance and collaboration. One of the family had been imprisoned for spreading Allied news, another had been smuggled out of Malaya, joined the British paratroops and jumped back to the guerrillas fighting the Japanese. Yet another of them had worked for the Japanese, distributing petrol rations, and was boasting over dinner of his black-market activities.

They talked of the collapse of the British when the Japanese appeared: how officers had deserted their men, and how, as the Japanese approached, two British officers had sat at the end of their road, dead drunk, pouring bottles of whisky over one another. They told us, too, of the arrogance of the British planters and officials before the war and how hollow and demoralised they had been in face of the Japanese. One of the women said, "If they behave like they did before the war there will be trouble."

That trouble was already looming. In Indo-China (Vietnam, Cambodia and Laos), the British army was suppressing the resistance movement to recover the area for the French, and using Japanese troops to do so, though we did not know that at the time. Our Brigade was soon to be sent to what is now called Indonesia, on behalf of the Dutch, to try to win it back from the Indonesian resistance. The empires were striking back. The nationalist movements, led by Communists or left-wing nationalists who had learned their politics in Paris, London, the Hague and Moscow, had fought against the Japanese and been encouraged to do so. Now they were being forcibly, even though not successfully, disarmed, disbanded and suppressed.

On our way up from Port Dickson to Kuala Lumpur, we had passed a large and well laid out encampment of the Malay Peoples' Anti-Japanese Army (MPAJA), with guards on duty dressed smartly in Chinese style unifoms, carrying light arms. Above flew a red flag with three gold stars, standing for the three main peoples of Malaya, the Malays, the Chinese and the Indians. This army, we were told, had been supported and encouraged by the British. In the towns it was backed by a political organisation, the Malay Peoples' Anti-Japanese Movement (MPAJM). When we arrived the MPAJA controlled most of the country; the Japanese held the larger towns but found it difficult to travel by day and impossible by night. Two of the Anti-Japanese Army leaders were to march in the Victory Parade in London.

We were forbidden to mention the MPAJA or MPAJM in our letters home. It was explained that the MPAJA was to be disarmed and disbanded and that these measures might lead to some conflict. We were not to worry what the Russians might think about this because these people were not "real Communists" like our Soviet allies, and had no connection with Russia. We were also told that there had been very little collaboration with the Japanese.

At once, a propaganda campaign began against the resistance movement. Every act of robbery or violence, in what was practically a lawless country, was blamed on the "Chinese Communists". The use of "Chinese" gave the effect of "alien". In fact, the Chinese had settled in Malaya long before the British. Many of the families had been in the peninsula for hundreds of years, some since the eleventh century. While, everywhere, Chinese culture was exclusive and traditional, the Malay Chinese did not think of themselves as belonging to China but as part of Malaya; while to the British, Britain was always "home". Since the Chinese formed the commercial and professional classes of Malaya, it was natural that they should be also the political class. Leaders of the political movement, the MPAJM, were targeted for silencing. Soon Kwong, secretary of the movement in Selangor State, was arrested and charged with extortion, for allegedly arresting and fining a Japanese agent responsible for a number of deaths. We were told that he had been extorting money from shopkeepers; but no such charge was brought. The court found him innocent, so he was rearrested and charged with the same offence (no nonsense about double jeopardy!) Again, he was found innocent; so he faced a third trial, was found guilty and went into prison. Than Huatt, secretary of the Malacca Communist Party, was warned that he would be arrested if he continued to make speeches demanding elections for a democratic government.

Two weeks after we arrived, we learned that our tanks were being used to intimidate striking coal miners, who were demanding a pay rise at a time of inflation, when their wages would scarcely buy one meal a day. We learned, also, that British Military Police, helped by plain clothes men who had worked for the Japanese, were rounding up "thieves" from the villages who were tapping rubber trees on overgrown plantations.

Those of us who felt indignation at what was happening told each other that the Labour Government could not know what was going on, and blamed the tin and rubber interests. We did not know that the economic strategy of our Government was to be based on selling Malayan, and other colonial, products to the USA for dollars, which Britain then used to buy goods from the USA. The value of the dollars was paid in sterling into sterling balances, frozen for many years, held in the Bank of England. In short, Malaya and other colonies were forced to lend their dollars to Britain in exchange for frozen pounds.

Many years later I told Malcolm Caldwell of the School of African and Oriental Studies, University of London, of these events. He sent a research student to the Public Record Office to look up the official papers covering this period in Malaya. The files were marked: "On permanent loan to T. Atkins". The army was holding on to its own historical events.

35 "Where there ain't no Ten Commandments" [12]

The streets of Malacca, to which we were moved in October, reflected the town's long history, from the time when it dominated the peninsula and the Straits: the Arab inspired Islam of the Malays, the homes of the Chinese, churches of the Portuguese, Dutch gabled houses from the eighteenth century, and the nineteenth century buildings of the British. It was interesting to wander round the town and look at shops which had lots of second-hand watches, looted successively from the British and the Japanese, but a choice of books limited by Catholic and British censorship and Japanese occupation.

We lived in a group of bungalows, which had belonged to wealthy Chinese, on a hill from which parkland took one to the city. Living in small groups of four to six in separate bungalows, scarcely supervised, allowed an unhappy turn of events. The place swarmed with young women, Malay and Chinese, offering themselves to British soldiers who for months and years had had few sexual outlets. Men brought women to their bungalows for the night, and the habit grew. One young wireless operator (WO) from Wembley had a different woman in each night, and grew pastier and pastier faced. Another, who was half-French, justified himself by saying that if he did this now he would be far more likely to be faithful to a wife later on!

Many of the young women had been "comfort girls" for the Japanese. Soon venereal diseases began to spread. A Scots WO who was a victim told of long queues of all ranks at the VD clinic.

The squadron was sharply divided by what was happening. Johnnie Dance, Lievesley and I banned women from our bungalow, and there were others who did the same. But we were in a minority. I argued that we were supposed to have come as "liberators", but that now we should be looked on, by most of the local people, with hostility. This was borne out when the Brigadier's driver was threatened and abused while taking a "taxi-girl" home from the dance hall, as he put it, "to do her a bit of good". At the dance hall you bought a book of tickets and gave them to partners who would dance with you. Many of the taxi girls were prostitutes.

It seemed to me that men who, only weeks beforehand had been arguing about politics and the sort of country they were going home to and were talking about their families, were now concerned only with the pleasures of unlimited and uninhibited sex. Perhaps I should have been more understanding of the problems and urges of my colleagues, but that was not how I felt at the time. It made no difference to our social relationships, but my views were regarded as odd.

There had been a whiff of this at Kuala Lumpur. The Captain had suggested that I lead a series of weekly discussions on post-war problems. We drew up a list of topics which he approved. Mistakenly I chose as the first discussion, "The Position of Women After the War", instead of something like housing, because it would lead to a good discussion. I suggested that women who had had jobs and incomes at war work, and had known some independence, would not want to go "back to the home", and that women would want equal pay with men. I was in a minority of three; angry views were expressed; Reg, the Transport Sergeant, said that a marriage where both husband and wife worked was "just a shagging match"! There were no more weekly discussions.

But there was to be a better scheme when we were in Malacca. The Army had started rehabilitation programmes, aimed at preparing service people for civilian life. At formation colleges run by the Army Education Corps, men and women could take the "forces prelim", which was accepted as matric, or could attend just for a liberal education. The Malaya Command was to set up three colleges, one of which would train instructors. I applied for the staff of one of the colleges, and to be transferred to the Education Corps.

The officers of our squadron said there was no reason why we should not be first. We held conferences of the unit to see what resources we had and what subjects people wanted and to plan syllabuses. We begged a few textbooks, wall maps and a blackboard from local schools and fixed up a classroom. We had eighteen-twenty periods a week, for maths, science and economics, geography and English literature. I took the economics; Johnnie Dance the maths and science. The scheme was very popular.

36 Darker Skies

Conflict in Malaya was becoming more and more likely, although the local left seemed optimistic. In my wanderings I came across the offices of the Malay People's Anti-Japanese Movement, and went in. Two men invited me to sit down and accepted me easily in spite of the uniform. A few days later we had a second meeting. They told me about the resistance and its operations. They thought there would have to be democratic elections from which the MPAJM would emerge as the largest group. Did I not know that in France and Italy the Communists were the largest party? I asked whether there had been Malay support for the MPAJA or whether it was virtually entirely Chinese. They said that there were some Malays among the leaders, and in the ranks, and that the guerrillas could not have existed in the jungle without the co-operation of Malay villagers. They invited me to come to the celebration of the anniversary of the Soviet Revolution on 7 November.

That afternoon almost every house in Malacca flew a red flag, and the shops shut. As I sat drinking coffee a column of the MPAJA came marching up the street and dispersed into the opera house, followed by a great crowd which I joined. A backcloth to the stage carried portraits of Marx, Lenin and Stalin; on the stage was a band surrounded by flowers. In the front row sat the guerrilla leaders, and those of the MPAJM and the Communist Party. When the men I had talked to saw me, they sent to invite me to join them, but that would have been folly, so I sat near the back. A Chinese girl gave me a yellow paper flower which for years I used as a bookmark. There were speeches, which brought the audience to its feet, but of which I understood not a word; the *International* and other revolutionary songs were rendered in Chinese by two choirs, there was a ceremony with banners which I could not fathom, and two plays. One graphically portrayed a family killing themselves because of Japanese oppression, the father coming home, finding them and going off to join the guerrillas. The other was a satire on the Japanese officers and their puppet administrators, which had the audience roaring with laughter. Outside, lightning played above the palm trees and thunder added to the drama of the darkening afternoon.

The mood was one of great confidence in the future. But the first blasts of what we later learned to call the Cold War were blowing. The USSR was clashing with the other allies over the structure of the United Nations: the newspapers were increasingly anti-Soviet. I had been optimistic that the British people would remain friendly to the Russians because of the war. But now I had doubts. The leading Soviet football team, Moscow Dynamo, came to Britain to play British teams and hostility followed. At first Dynamo was very popular and the newspapers were enthusiastic about its goalkeeper, "Tiger" Komitch. This lasted until the last match, the key game with Arsenal. There was a fog, one end of the pitch was invisible from the other. Arsenal wanted to cancel. Dynamo stupidly refused. Even more foolishly, there was a Russian referee. The teams scored equally, until he gave a penalty against Arsenal, Dynamo scored and won. The crowd and the press declared it was a fix. Friendship began to evaporate. I knew then that the political climate was growing cold.

37 To the Mountains

I woke up with a high fever, and was taken to Malacca Hospital. The doctors called it "NYD Fever" – Not Yet Diagnosed, the most common ailment in the East. The cause was poor feeding in a hot, damp and sapping climate. We had not had a good meal since Ahmednagar, where our wonder cook, Bill, had gone home to be demobilised. We had lived on tinned army food and only a few days before I was ill we had begun to receive bread and a few local supplies – a kind of runner bean and mouldy sweet potatoes.

The fever lasted a week and departed after treatment with M & B, an early penicillin product. During the week Johnnie Dance had joined me with his dose of NYD. The MO, a warm and pleasant man who talked to his charges, decided that I should go on convalescent leave to the Cameron Highlands, a pre-war mountain resort of the Sahibs. However, while waiting for my permit and rail pass I should remain in the hospital, not rejoin the unit where I would have to work and eat poor food. I looked forward to a real rest. Meanwhile Johnnie and I talked and read. The hospital was a splendid building, comfortable and well equipped, certainly superior to anything I had seen in India, as were the other social services, including education, in Malaya.

The three hundred mile train journey was slow, the train crowded with peasants. Among us were two Dutch settlers, large men in white shorts and shirts who lounged arrogantly over several seats. They said they had been Japanese prisoners, but looked well fed and prosperous, quite unlike the skeletal figures then being released from the camps. The Dutch were very unpopular in South East Asia and the Malays and Chinese on the train kept well away from these two, although they wedged themselves on the seat with me, in spite of my uniform.

At the station for the Highlands I was loaded into the back of a 30 cwt. truck, which swung sickeningly round hairpin bends and alongside sharp drops in the jungle road which climbed the six thousand feet to the resort. There, what had been a hotel was sparsely but comfortably furnished. It was warm on the cold nights, with tolerable food. A gramophone seemed to be endlessly playing a record of Mary Martin singing "Do it Again, Please Do it Again".

There was a one-street town in which I found a second-hand bookshop and, on the shelves, an Everyman edition of *Robinson Crusoe*. "How much?" I asked the Malay bookseller. He told me that his little girl was ill and could not get milk. I could have the book for a tin of milk. I cajoled or bribed the cook into giving me two tins of Carnation milk. The book is still on my shelf.

The greatest pleasure was to walk along the paths into the jungle, where grew an amazing variety of ferns, from tiny moss ferns to tall tree-ferns. It was easy to see how Alfred Russell Wallace, working in the Malay archipelago, had found evidence to develop his theories of evolution through natural selection at the same time as Darwin.

Blessed rest! I was beginning to enjoy the relaxation, the quietness and the opportunity of solitude, when a message arrived: I was to return to the squadron immediately, from where I would go for a month's leave in England, flying home in time for Christmas.

38 Home for Christmas!

It was called LIAP. Each unit could choose one person to go first for a month at home. Most of our squadron were expecting early demob and did not apply. I wasn't, and was chosen on the grounds that Mother had died. I was to join other lucky applicants at Singapore for the air-lift. There I met three friends who had been at Ballymena and Norfolk and on the Maloja. We were told that there was no plane, so we would fly from Calcutta,

We waited four days, playing bridge and Monopoly, and walking to Singapore with its overcrowded slums, to go to the cinema, where we saw

The Long Voyage Home, the film of O'Neill's Glencairn plays, an American film with Dutch subtitles at a Chinese cinema in a British colony.

So, we were on a crowded troopship. The food was disgusting. There were some tough, coarse and boastful long-service men on board, going home for demob. They took the food and threw it at the cook, after which there was a slight improvement. We wound up the treacherous channels of the Hoogli to the Calcutta docks and were taken to a large transit camp.

There we learned that we would not be home for Christmas. There was "fog in England" and planes could not take off. Had we been told that the planes were needed to take POWs from the Japanese camps, or men of the 14th Army, home, we would have believed and accepted it – but "fog"! Or was it because of the developing confrontation with the USSR?

This meant another Christmas in a transit camp, with tinned turkey and tinned Christmas pudding served by officers to men they did not know. In the new year we began a four-day train journey across India, in third class carriages, with slatted wooden seats and luggage racks, and with one hole in the floor for each carriage-load of fifty or sixty men. It was difficult to lie down except on the floor, some slept on the luggage racks. Our small group played bridge the whole way: I have never played since.

At Bombay we joined the P & O liner Strathnaver. Our lives became relatively luxurious: little of the troopship atmosphere remained. The ship was not crowded. It carried not only returning "other ranks", but also Indian Army officers with their wives and administrators "going home" with theirs. The food was excellent and the climate perfect. There was a cruise atmosphere, with sweepstakes on how far the ship would travel in the day; in the evenings there were film shows or concerts. I particularly remember a piano recital by a Sergeant, Dr Cook, who was a concert pianist: a large audience filled the saloon deck, sitting in silence while he played a Beethoven sonata, among other works. There were quizzes and "brains trusts". At one of these I was one of the team, sitting next to a real memsahib. I still recall her anger when we were asked what we thought of the Hindu doctrine of reincarnation.

The Mediterranean was calm and warm, so was Biscay. Then, on the blowy night of 7 February, we lined the rails as we entered the Channel and picked up the lights, one by one – Land's End, the Lizard, the Eddystone, Start Point, Portland and the Needles. Then we dropped anchor in Southampton Water. I spent four weeks with my family and friends in Bridport and London, and was able to visit Harry Welford in the TB sanatorium. Then, one March morning, I found myself on a very cold airfield near Cambridge.

39 Join the Army – See the World

My friends from the journey home and I, with others returning to India, boarded a Liberator, the second largest type of the US bomber, now owned by the RAF. We sat in the bomb bay and hoped that the pilot would not press the wrong button. At Paris we moved up into the body of the plane and could see the French countryside, le pont d'Avignon, and the great circle of mud at the mouths of the Rhone.

We were aiming for Tunis, but half way across the Mediterranean the pilot remembered that there was a dance at the RAF station at Istres, so, announcing that he had a cold, he turned the plane round and landed at Istres, a small town between Marseilles and the Pyrenees, painted in Mediterranean colours with a small bull ring of baked earth painted pink.

It seemed that the whole town had come to the dance; old women in shawls, old men on sticks, men and women in black, small children in boots and long black stockings. When refreshments were announced it was clear why they had come: they rose as one and fell upon the food. In a few minutes it had all gone. In the aftermath of the war, the South of France was poor and hungry.

Next day the pilot was "well enough" to fly to Tunis. We had not time to visit Carthage, but Tunis itself was fascinating, and in the bright sunlight the classical statues looked warm and alive, very unlike those in the British Museum. That evening, the four of us ate in a restaurant where the muscular waitress demonstrated by rather obvious gestures what effect the chillies and peppers in the dish would have on us.

Next day we flew over the desert, littered with wrecked vehicles and burnt-out tanks, all the left over rubbish of war. We landed at an airstrip about a mile from the Pyramids. No one wanted to go with me, so I walked across the desert and explored the great monuments, not then a popular tourist attraction. At the Sphinx a tout offered me a "coin of Queen Cleopatra". I was willing to buy a fraud as a souvenir and kept it for many years. As darkness fell, a full moon rose over the desert and turned the whole site into a magic place of light and long shadows. Others thought so too, for couples appeared and, climbing onto the huge stone blocks of the Pyramids, settled down for an evening of embraces.

We explored Cairo, and hated it. The poverty seemed even more sordid than that of India. The city had been the centre of military activity for so long that it carried an atmosphere of corruption. Touts and beggars pestered us and a legion of small boys aggressively demanded to clean our boots. One threw liquid blacking over our feet and then demanded money to wipe it off.

We flew over Arabia to Basra, then on to Bombay, where the four of us said good-bye to each other. There was plenty of time in Bombay to call at the Raj Bhavan and see Mohan. There was a feeling of excitement following strikes over the slowness of demob at RAF stations in India, and unrest and protests in the British and Indian forces in South East Asia.[13] There was even a mutiny of Gurkhas over the quality of their boots – the Indian Navy in Bombay, Karachi and elsewhere had mutinied on 18 February and been backed by some Indian Army technical units. It was reported that the ships had trained their guns on the Taj Mahal Hotel, equivalent to the Ritz. The Communist Party had called a general strike in Bombay, in support of the sailors. A demonstration of several million people had surged through the city, headed by the linked flags of Congress, Muslim League and the CPI. The nationalist leaders as well as the British were horrified. The police had killed more than two hundred people in restoring order in Bombay and the Congress strong man Vallabhai Patel had come to Bombay to persuade the sailors to surrender. There had been a general election from which Congress and the Muslim League had emerged as the two strong forces in the country, with the CPI winning a number of seats in the rural and industrial constituencies.

But the unity between the members of the parties during the mutiny was not shared by the leaders, who breathed fire at each other. Jinnah had shouted, "Pakistan or death!", and Patel had bawled back, "We will shed our blood before we grant Pakistan." Mohan's estimate was that the British would impose the division of India and there would be civil war.

From Bombay I was flown in a Dakota – the small type transport plane built in the US and reputed to be unsafe – over the Western Ghats to Poona. There I visited Izzy Pushkin who was teaching at the formation college. We had long talks about news from home and from India.

The last stage of my journey was in another Dakota, which lived up to its reputation when a window fell out as we flew across the dried brown Deccan, its patchwork of fields and dusty roads looking like a Picasso. To step from the plane at Madras was to enter a steam bath and a world of colour. If the Deccan had been Picasso, Madras was Gauguin – blue, white and yellow blossom, the fierce colours of the clothes and streets.

There I was to await a boat to Jakarta, where the squadron was helping the Dutch attempt to take Java back from its people. The transit camp was unspeakable, so I moved to the Toc H hostel where I rented a room which had a comfortable bed with cool, clean sheets, a bathroom and a fan, and where I could buy good meals. A selection of SE Asian camps had convinced me that, with a few exceptions, those who ran them were either inefficient or corrupt, or both.

Each day I reported to the Transport Officer to ask about a ship. One day he said, "Your unit is returning to India. They land here this afternoon." So I sat on the dockside and waited. Presently the ship appeared, docked and made fast. Down the gangway came my companions, astonished to see me on the quayside, and full of warm greetings. It was almost a family reunion.

40 Politically Unreliable

The Brigade had been declared "politically unreliable", and was to be disbanded. Over a meal in a Chinese restaurant my friends told the story. The best of our three battalions had not been taken to Java because it was already politically disaffected. In Java, Indian troops had begun to desert. Two of my friends, one a *havildar* (Indian Army Sergeant) had disappeared with a jeep, radio set and their small arms. The British troops had hated the campaign: their attitude was "what the hell has this got to do with us?" They claimed that they were more in danger from the trigger-happy Dutch than from the Indonesians.

Two days later I had to leave my Toc H retreat and journey with the squadron to Secunderabad, a "modern", and largely military, town near Hyderabad. Hyderabad itself was the capital of the largest of the Native States, ruled over by the Nizam, a Moslem prince of a mainly Hindu state, and reputed to be one of the world's richest men. Among other sources of income he received one anna a year for every coconut palm in the state, and there were millions. His palace was guarded by Kremlin-like walls. Hyderabad was the only place in India where stones were thrown at us by young men shouting "*Jai Hind*" ("Quit India").

At Secunderabad we waited for weeks. We went into large stone barracks cooled by *punkhas* and we idled or paraded. Morale was almost at rock bottom. I had not done a job for five months. All the majority of the squadron seemed interested in apart from demob was any opportunity for sex. The educational scheme planned in Malacca had collapsed. The CO took no interest in us. The food, supplied by the firm of Motiram, which had robbed the troops since Kipling's day, was unacceptable. We did not accept it. Twenty minutes queuing for breakfast brought two over-boiled eggs, one of which was probably bad. We preferred to pay the "fried egg wallah" outside six annas (2 1/2 pence) for two good fried eggs. Each time the Catering Officer approached the squadron's tables we complained. An inquiry showed that the cook house was drawing rations for ninety men under strength. After that he did not ask us if we had any complaints.

It was impossible that British troops, if we were anything to go by, could be used to hold on to India, still less to fight a war against the Soviet Union, though the new generation of conscripts coming out had not been in the war and had a different view of the world. Verbal conflicts between the Soviet government and ours were reported every day. The Russians were negotiating a treaty with Persia (Iran) to obtain an oil concession. They had occupied the northern half of the country during the war, while Britain occupied the south, and the country was used to rush supplies to the eastern front. The press had talked of a "Russian invasion" and some Moslem nationalist leaders were banking on war. Jinnah had said the Britain should grant Pakistan to provide a friendly base from which to protect India. Firoz Khan Noon, Premier of the Punjab, added: "If Britain will not give us Pakistan, Russia will." (The Soviet Union withdrew troops from Persia and was promised an oil concession, which a year later was cancelled).

At last relief came with the end of the 50th Indian Armoured Brigade. The Captain told us that we could share out the books in the unit library, three each. It was the first that any of us had heard of the library. Some were not interested in books so would sell their share for fifty cigarettes. I ended up with nine.

We hired a room at a Chinese restaurant where we had a farewell meal followed by a social evening of songs and speeches. I felt pangs at saying goodbye to friends, but relieved that I was now to be occupied – or so I thought. I had asked to be transferred as a teacher at the sub-area school. This was in a large house in the countryside outside Secunderabad. In its garden was a flame of the forest tree, its bright red blossom a contrast to the arid fields around. I moved to a small house where lived about a dozen Signal Sergeants, half a mile from the school. Because it was a Sergeants' mess, I had to assume the rank and wear three stripes – but without Sergeants' pay. Our rooms, apart from a few in the house, were the former servants' quarters, small compartments on a concrete platform around a courtyard. They were partly open at the front, but not uncomfortable. Not far behind the buildings was a massive rock, rising a hundred and fifty feet out of the earth, worn round and smooth so that it resembled a great breast of an Earth goddess. On top was a tiny nipple of a temple. I was warned not to try the path to the top, because scorpions and snakes lived in the crevices of the rock.

Captain James, who was in charge, showed me round the school. He was proud of his building, its equipment and library. I asked how many students there were; he said there were no students. This did not seem to bother him, so I suggested sending a notice to all the many units in the area, inviting applications. Rather reluctantly he agreed. There was an Education Corps Sergeant in charge of administration helped by a Eurasian clerk, and a woman officer of the WAC(I) (Women's Auxiliary Corps India). So they all administered whatever it was they were administering, and I, once again, sat in my well-equipped room, reading.

41 Politically Unacceptable

The WAC officer asked, "Why do you sit in your room all day, reading?" "Because I have no students." She revealed that she had a few dozen young women asking for classes, but had no teacher. Captain James had not thought of bringing us together. Would I teach them English, elocution, current affairs and "How to instruct"? Doubtful about elocution, I agreed. The young women were nearly all Eurasian, surrounded by prejudices and with little education. Asked what they wished to do after the army, all said, "To get married if I have a suitable offer."

Attendance was not good. Frequently their officers would not release them, or transport to the school failed to appear; but those who came for an hour each afternoon were enthusiastic and I enjoyed our sessions. By the end of May the school came to life. To my joy, Johnnie Dance arrived to teach maths and science. A young art teacher came also. Then twenty-one British soldiers arrived for a month's full-time study, in preparation for their forces matric. I had large classes in English, general knowledge, history and economics. Though many of them had little education, the students were keen and inclined to the left – one had been a Labour councillor in Harrow. It was good, after so much idleness, to be almost overworked with teaching twenty sessions a week, preparation and commenting on written work.

The only shadows were those cast by army stupidity. We were told to move our billets because we were working for the sub-area school, not for the sub-area – that suggestion was defeated. Captain James had no ideas about education in his head. "I don't want your opinion", he snapped when

Letter of the Week

H. FYRTH, 3 Coy. Signals, 172 (Secunderabad) Sub-Area:

IN your issue of April 25 I have just read an article on Greece in which appears the statement "There was general agreement that the results of the election (of March 31) were a pretty fair reflection of the mood of the Greek people."

This looks like one of those delightful journalistic phrases used to hide facts and not reveal them. It may mean several things, but if it means that the Government elected represents the "mood of the Greek people" I am afraid it hardly corresponds with the truth. These are the facts.

The elections were fixed by the British Government for March 31, and in spite of many requests Mr. Bevin would not postpone them. The EAM parties (the Socialists, Communists, Left Liberals and Union of Democratic Clubs) therefore decided to boycott the elections on the grounds (a) that the election registers were false, and (b) that Royalist and Fascist terror was running wild in the country.

On February 27 the "Daily Herald" reported: "The Greek Cabinet is now unanimously in favour of postponement". The Cabinet represented all parties except the EAM.

In March, fourteen out of the 36 Cabinet Ministers resigned as a protest against the undemocratic nature of the elections, stating that four-fifths of the police, judiciary and army officers belonged to the Fascist-Monarchist "X" organisation.

The elections themselves have fully justified the decision of the EAM. The report of the Allied election observers, signed on April 11 by the British, American and French heads of the Mission, stated that 29 per cent of the electoral lists were "invalid or of doubtful validity."

On March 27 the Athens correspondent of the "Manchester Guardian" wrote: "The voters number 2,200,000 of whom nearly 500,000 are 'dead'."

It is easy to see that under conditions of terrorism a number of 'dead' people could easily vote.

Reporters on the spot testified that Right Wing terrorism was unbridled. Peter Burchett, "Daily Express" correspondent, wrote on the election eve: "Since yesterday evening there has been a wave of arrests of EAM supporters . . Those distributing leaflets asking the people to abstain from voting are immediately beaten up by the police"

Argyris, Athens reporter of the "Christian Science Monitor," wrote: "Fairly clear proof exists that approximately one-quarter of the Leftists in the large cities voted under duress. Many Leftist Government workers of Salonika voted in order to protect their jobs; also many factory workers similarly were compelled to vote."

Such were the conditions of Greek "democracy." Yet in spite of terrorism the final result showed that 55 per cent of the electorate abstained from voting, following the lead of the EAM. Of the parties taking part, the extreme Right emerged slightly larger than any other party and has, therefore, formed a Cabinet backed by a minority of the people.

Prime Minister Poulityas held the position of President of the Supreme Court in German-occupied Greece. Minister of the Interior Theatokis returned to Greece with the Germans, bringing a personal letter from Marshal List. Minister of Communications Gonotas helped to organise the Security Battalions under German rule.

Is it not clear in view of these facts that the new Greek Government in no way "reflects the mood of the Greek people"? And is it not equally clear that the Greek set-up is a serious threat to democracy and to the peace now in its very delicate infancy?

In short, isn't our Government backing a very dangerous horse in Greece?

'Letter of the Week' in Forces newspaper 'Contact', 30th May 1946. Didn't cause trouble?

I had ventured it. He told Johnnie off for saying that the English educational system perpetuated class divisions, because "the Colonel would not like it." Johnnie's statement was from a War Office pamphlet we had. One day the two of us with a dozen students passed a Brigadier's car without saluting. He came roaring towards us bellowing, swearing, fuming and threatening to "run us in". He made us each salute in turn. We all had a good laugh when he left.

The summer grew hotter, the fields more parched. The only colours in the landscape were the flame of the forest and the dusty green tops of the Banyan trees. The only living creature seemed to be the coppersmith bird, whose note sounded "tonk-tonk-tonk" all day. (It was also known as the "Doolalli" bird because it drove soldiers mad.) The walk to the mess at lunchtime became more and more of a trudge.

At last the monsoon broke. Huge clouds piled up, flashes of lightning were followed by pouring rain. We all ran out of the mess, shedding our clothes and rejoiced in the water. The next morning the earth was covered by a film of green. Within a week the grass was a foot high. The insects swarmed. At night, mosquitoes, monsoon flies and beetles crashed into my lamp. Creatures came alive. On the fence a slow moving chameleon flicked its tongue to catch insects. The Eurasian clerk invited Johnnie and me to a double christening party. His wife and her sister both had babies and we met the extended families for a large spread. They seemed to think that two babies called for twice as much, poor quality, drink. We returned to the mess, our arms round each other, feeling that we were walking on the tops of the Banyan trees. We suffered.

Another social engagement was more decorous. It was with A R Chari, a friend of Mohan. He had introduced me to the local leaders of the railway union, who gave me the facts about workers' wages that lay behind the threat of a national strike. I also met some of his comrades who drew a grim picture of political life in Hyderabad – far worse than in British India. Progressive leaders were frequently confined to their villages or arrested and subjected to the kind of torture more associated with the Japanese.

Chari said, "Will you come and take a little rice with me?" The invitation was for 8.30, and, not understanding what "a little rice" meant, I had my early evening meal at the mess. At Chari's we talked on the veranda until 10.30, when his wife put before us the largest and hottest curry I have ever eaten. The duty of a guest forced it down. His wife did not join us.

The end of this pleasant and fruitful life came suddenly. Johnnie had gone home to be demobbed, when Captain James summoned me to his office to tell me that a new Intelligence Officer had arrived in the sub-area, had looked through my file and said, in effect, "I'm not having this man teaching in my parish." I was to gather my belongings and leave the school at once, to return to Mhow as soon as could be arranged.

Perhaps it was the letter, but that had been two months earlier. Weekly newspapers were published for the forces. The Indian one was *Contact*, the South-East Asian SEAC. They contained news from Britain and abroad and lively controversies. They were progressive, edited by Frank Owen, a socialist friend of Michael Foot and his predecessor as editor of the *Evening Standard*. There had been an article on the erupting crisis in Greece, which said that recent elections represented the mood of the people. I wrote a letter pointing out that the Allied appointed observers and the British and American correspondents had reported that the elections were rigged and took place in an atmosphere of fascist and monarchist terror, with the majority of electors boycotting the poll. The letter had appeared in *Contact* as "Letter of the Week", spread across two columns. The IO may have seen it. Whatever his reasons, I was once more waiting for a railway ticket.

Yet the best laid plans of IOs sometimes run into the sand. The sweeper came to me and said, "The Sahib is very ill." A young Sergeant had taken to his bed feeling unwell. Now he had a high fever and was in distress. Being alone in the mess, I sent for a truck. We lifted him into the back, wrapped in a blanket. On the way to the hospital I sat cradling him in my arms, trying to comfort him. At the hospital a doctor came and told us that he had poliomyelitis and had been put into the iron lung. That evening the senior Sergeant took me outside and said the boy had died. The world reeled. He went on to say that I was now in quarantine and was to "report sick" at the least symptom.

So for the next weeks I was confined to my room, reading, writing articles on the impending railway strike for *The Railway Review* (organ of the National Union of Railwaymen) and the newspapers and working out some economic ideas. I wrote to the boy's parents. He had been thought cocky and was not popular, but I sang his virtues and told them just what happened. Their reply was sad, he was the only child of older parents, but they were full of gratitude that he had gone to a good hospital as they had pictured neglect in the wilds. They invited me to visit them when I was home, but I could never face it. Then the rail-pass arrived.

42 The Bullshit Boys

Like the grace of God, the mind of Army Intelligence passeth all understanding. Declared unfit to teach adult soldiers in Secunderabad, I was put in charge of the education of the two dozen fifteen-to-seventeen year olds of the Boys' Company (Signals Training Centre) at Mhow.

To me the idea of turning children into regular soldiers was revolting. They had been born and grown up in barracks, sons of regulars and Indian or Eurasian women, many of them with dark skins, which did not inhibit their racism. They were being robbed of childhood and turned into automata whose horizons were the barrack and the brothel, recognising only two types of person, martinets to be obeyed and avoided and "softies" to be walked over. All were larger and heavier than I was. Their exactness in drill equalled that of the Guards, their kit was meticulous, and their football skills were a pleasure to watch. But their behaviour was that of naughty eight-year-olds. At close quarters they were exasperating, but I liked them – some of them very much – and was sad for them, especially for those who did not wish to be soldiers.

Perhaps Intelligence was not so daft, for what was possible for me was ringed by restrictions. The syllabus laid down was made up of history – using a book called *The Soldier and the Empire*, geography "to be taught from a Military and Imperial viewpoint", English grammar and maths with problems of the "if one column of marching men starts from A ..." variety. My first job was to see the CO, a Captain who was a lawyer from High Wycombe and whom I had known as a Lance Corporal at Catterick. He seemed an unlikely officer for his job, as became clear when he sometimes invited me for a drink and talk of an evening. He agreed that I jettison the syllabus and make my own: no history, human geography, basic maths, English through reading books and writing short stories, basic science and current affairs alternating each week and a monthly review of the news.

Even so, the older boys were due for an exam in October and must not fail. And there were obstacles from the boys themselves: a list of novels, mainly adventure stories, was brought back to me by a group who said the Catholic priest had forbidden them to read *The Three Musketeers* or *The Count of Monte Cristo*, because Dumas was on the Index. The lesson when I told them about Darwin was a near riot: it was insulting to suggest that they had any link with animals.

But the biggest barrier was their dislike of education. Asked at our first meeting whether they thought learning English was a waste of time, they shouted that all education was a waste of time and, to back up their views, banged their desks or stood on them, threw chairs and broke an overhead lampshade. The Sergeant, who insisted on being there "to keep order", shouted that they would be on a charge and thumped the table with his cane. I told him to stop and quietened them by talking loudly and looking the ringleaders in the eye. The OC agreed that the Sergeant should not be there and that they be divided into two classes for a time. Gradually they listened and took part in discussion – something new to them. We became friends.

Even so, the Army is the Army. A Corporal Arthur arrived, a regular who had been offered leave in Britain but who said he was not happy away from barracks. He was a fascist; when I saw him reading *Mein Kampf* and asked him why, he replied that he liked Hitler's ideas about militarism and race. He thought everything too slack and decreed that the boys polish the bottoms of their mess tins and also the spare fly-buttons from their hussifs, but one very rude word from me cancelled the latter order. He then told the OC that education was a waste of time and should be stopped.

The Captain called for me and I told Corporal Arthur what I thought of him and regular army ways and the Captain sided with me. One of the boys came in twenty minutes late for roll call, wearing civvies. Corporal Arthur put him on a charge and, because he had been in trouble before, he was discharged, more or less dishonourably. His last night was spent in the cells, expecting his father to beat him up when he arrived home.

It was a full life; at 5.15 a.m. the telephone in my room rang to call me; at 5.30 I called the boys; the day's work lasted until teatime at 5 p.m. Every third night I was on duty until 10 p.m. lights out. It would have been lonely but that some old friends from the squadron, and from other places, were around and we walked the ten miles to Patelpani and back some Sundays; the falls were in full spate and worth the long walk. I managed music night sometimes.

Gradually it was possible to make some progress with a few of the boys. Four of them went with me to see the American film of *Pride and Prejudice*, enjoyed it and read the book afterwards. One of them confided that he hated the idea of being a soldier and wished to be a journalist, like Rudyard Kipling. I did all I could to support and encourage him. We started a wall newspaper with himself as the editor. It carried sports reports and articles about sportsmen and whatever he could persuade his fellows to write about. He really enjoyed the evenings when the two of us made up the newspaper. The OC agreed that we start a debating society; the standard was not high, but it was something. I arranged three sessions of sex education. At the first we discussed relations between men and women with me stressing equality of the sexes. Surprisingly the discussion was very good and they were ready to discuss calmly the idea of women as their equals. The second, also a success, was on reproduction and birth control, since they knew a lot about intercourse, but nothing about conception and birth. The third was about family relationships and prostitution.

Then, just as I began to feel a slight sense of achievement, NYD fever struck again.

43 Peace, Murder and a Sudden End

After the endless demands of the barracks, hospital had all the pleasures of a retreat; quietness, relaxation, good food and, since M & B soon did its work, plenty of time for reading. When the *Kitabb wallah* came round with his box of books I bought *Sons and Lovers* and *The Return of the Native*. He then tried to persuade me to add *The Escapades of Erotic Edna* and the like, saying, "These are good, but I tell you that there is nothing in those you have bought, absolutely nothing."

The Army did not return a soldier straight from hospital to his unit; there was the red tape of "re-posting". So I spent a night in a barrack room with fearsome *punkhas* – the old type of long strips of heavy cloth, but worked by electricity and creating a typhoon of cold air. Lying under my mosquito net I became aware of the orderly, who had told me he was writing to his wife, talking to the little tea-boy, and the urgent protests of the child "Nai, Sahib, nai, nai, Sahib". I emerged, suspecting what is now called child abuse, the child fled and the shamefaced young man pleaded with me, "Well, it's all right. These people have a different sense of morality from ours."

The small successes and large frustrations of Boys' Company continued. I felt it would be cowardice in the face of the enemy to ask for posting. Personal frustration was increased as the carrot of demob was, like the donkey's incentive, continually moved further away.

But worse things were happening outside. I was given two days in Bombay. Jinnah had declared a Pakistan Day; aggressive speeches in Calcutta had led to attacks on Hindus and five thousand corpses on the street. The murder spread. At Victoria Terminus I asked a taxi driver to take me to the Raj Bhavan. He would take me only to the end of Sandhurst Road because the road was in a Hindu area, he was a Moslem and we would not be safe. At the Commune all was confusion. The previous day the children had seen a Hindu mob butcher a Moslem on the other side of the road, and they were acutely distressed.

Mohan was in despair, saying that only weeks earlier Moslems and Hindus in Bombay had been united in support of the naval mutiny and opposition to the British; now there was no chance of unity. He was right, these events were a curtain-raiser for the greater tragedy to come. Also we differed over the captured leaders of the Indian National Liberation Army. I thought they should be tried, he said "No", that would never be understood by the majority of Indians who looked on them as patriots. It was my last and saddest visit to Bombay.

He gave me the address of a Second Lieutenant Landa who had been called up after graduating at Reading and who was younger than me. Landa, who lived in West London, had Czech parents, and was now at Mhow. We spent evenings and Sundays together when we could. One week we set out to spend the day walking in the Vindhya Mountains but were driven back to the cinema by late monsoon rain. On another we cycled into the country to spend the day with Professor Ghosh, Vice Principal of the Holkar State College. He was a gentle, warm man, of left wing views, who welcomed us with affection.

Landa would regale me with stories of his officers' mess: how a yogi had demonstrated his skills, supporting a garden roller on his chest, or stopping the pulse in one wrist at a time, while MOs monitored his heart beat and blood pressure, and how he had promised to demonstrate walking on water; how the mess had agreed to take the *Daily Worker*, provided *Horse and Hound* was taken as a counter-balance; how the Colonel, entertaining another Colonel, spent the whole of dinner discussing anxiously the squatting of Kensington flats by homeless families.

We went to the bazaar where he helped me choose two carpets and offered to have them sent home with his kit by Cox & King's, the carriers to Anglo-India.

Suddenly, it all ended. I had seen in *Contact* a notice saying that servicemen with firsts in economics could apply for a post with the Economic Section of the Cabinet Secretariat. It seemed a long shot, but I applied, expecting nothing. But teleprinters in Delhi and Mhow started clicking and the CO summoned me to say the he had been instructed that Lance Corporal Fyrth was to be ready within twenty four hours to go to London for interview.

Never had forms been filled or rail passes issued so quickly; never had so much respect been shown to a Lance Corporal by higher ranks. Packing was done, farewells made and I was put on a train with two of the boys who were going on leave and who tried to prevent an Indian from entering our carriage, until I told them off. It was my last attempt to battle with their attitudes.

44 VIP. A Farewell to Empire

The train did not hurry, lumbering across what is now Pakistan and through the Thar Desert with its camels in place of bullock carts. At Karachi a Major and a Captain were waiting to take my luggage, bundle me into a car and drive to the harbour. A launch took me out to a Sunderland flying boat which was due in Poole Harbour the next day.

The Sunderland was both beautiful and luxurious. As we took off, great plumes of water rose on either side. Each passenger had an individual seat, with a table between two of us. Opposite me sat Brigadier Fitzroy MacLean, who had led the British Mission to Tito. I had read that he was touring the Far East to report on the morale of British troops, but the report which he was writing was about the Communist parties in each of the countries he had visited.

We stopped at Barra and then flew over the Arabian Desert, at only a few thousand feet. The flying boat was rocked and pitched by the rising hot air. Air sickness proved even more unpleasant than sea sickness. At Cairo we landed on the Nile and were taken to a houseboat for dinner and a chance to bath.

We took off about 11 p.m. and soon noticed that the outer starboard engine was on fire. The pilot explained that he would re-land, but must first fly round until the fuel load was lightened. A Sergeant began to panic, but was soon calmed. Round about midnight the plane landed on the Nile, full as the river was of hazardous rubbish, smoothly and calmly.

Taken to a hotel for the night, we were told to hold ourselves ready to restart when the plane was repaired. In the morning I went into the city to buy presents, and found that the flying boat had gone without me. I was put into an ordinary BOAC plane. We landed briefly at Malta, looking so small from the air that we seemed bound to miss the landing field, and Paris. Then London: peering at the lights, the Sergeant who had panicked said, "Caw! Just think of all those people eating fish and chips down there!" Heathrow was then an infant airport. The orange lights of the Great West Road led to the Great Midland Hotel in Marylebone Road, at that time an army staging post. In the Great War it had been a hospital where Mother visited Father in 1919.

I shared a room with an aggressive little regular. As we unpacked he took a leather pouch from his pocket and poured half a dozen rubies into his palm. They would, he said, set him up in "Civvy Street". I asked him where he got them and he told me that when he was searching houses for arms in Malaya he had taken them off a Chinese man. In response to my expression of shock he replied, "Well, probably he had stolen them." Had the man protested? "If he had I would have shot him."

It was my last image of the British Empire. In the morning I walked out into the October sunshine of the Marylebone Road.

* * *

Fortunately I was not appointed to the Economic Section.

In 1948 India and Pakistan became independent. The final division of the sub-continent was carried out with fatal haste and demarcation of the frontier drawn up by a Whitehall civil servant with little experience of India. In the Punjab, the most disputed area, Sikhs attacked Muslims, in the wave of what would nowadays be called ethnic cleansing and genocide, millions of Hindus, Muslims and Sikhs were driven across the new frontiers: a million were butchered. It was one of the greatest tragedies of the century.

In the same year an unrepresentative constitution was imposed on Malaya. The Communist Party foolishly withdrew five thousand men into the jungle, in the vain belief that the British could be defeated in the same way as the Japanese. After a five year emergency costing millions of pounds, and involving the use of Dyak head-hunters and the erection of "concentration" villages, from which the inhabitants were let out only to work, the remaining jungle fighters surrendered.

Within twenty years the British Empire, like those of other European powers, had almost ceased to exist.

Notes

1. For Ian Taylor's part as a messenger in the 1946 RAF strikes see David Duncan, *Mutiny in the RAF,* Socialist History Society, London, 1998.
2. Bill Carritt (1908-1999), youth leader, soldier, Communist candidate Westminster 1945 General Election, Westminster City Councillor 1945-9, squatters' organiser 1946, lecturer, poet.
3. Harry Welford (1921-1998), engineering shop steward, tenants' organiser, campaigner for NHS.
4. Subhas Chandra Bose. Former Congress Youth leader, worked with Japanese, formed the Indian National Liberation Army (INLA) made up of Indian POWs to fight British in Burma. Killed in plane crash in September 1945 shortly after VJ day. The myth grew that he had led the INLA to Delhi and driven the British from India.
5. For details of the Meerut Trial, see Jean Jones, *The League Against Imperialism*, SHS, London, 1996.
6. Congress Socialist Party (CSP) a leftist nationalist party, which in the 1940s advocated an uprising against the British.
7. Wartime slogan, Ministry of Information.
8. Foreman of Signals. A technical rank, equal in seniority to Sergeant Major.
9. Long March (1934-5). Epic migration of Chinese Communists and their Red Army from Kiangsi Provonce, where they were under attack from Chiang-Kai-Shek, to Yenan, 800 miles to the north-west.
10. See Patrick French, *Liberty or Death, India's journey to Independence and Division*, Harper Collins, London, 1997, for an account of the movements and negotiations leading to independence and partition.
11. Rabindranath Tagore (1861-1941), Bengali writer, poet, philosopher and educationalist, leader of Bengal Renaissance; founded cultural centre at Santiniketan. Awarded Nobel Prize for Literature, 1913.
12. Chapter title, Rudyard Kipling, *The Road to Mandalay*.
13. See David Duncan, *op. cit.*

THE SOCIALIST HISTORY SOCIETY

The Socialist History Society was founded 10 years ago and includes among its members many of this country's leading Socialist and labour historians. We have a growing membership of both academics and others who might consider themselves amateur historians. The SHS holds regular events, public meetings and one-off conferences, and contributes to current historical debates and controversies. The society produces a range of publications, including the journal *Socialist History*. We can sometimes assist with individual student research.

The SHS is the successor to the Communist Party History Group, established in 1946. The society is now independent of all political parties and groups. We are engaged in and seek to encourage historical studies from a Marxist and broadly-defined left perspective. We are concerned with every aspect of human history from early social formations to the present day and aim for a global reach.

We are particularly interested in the struggles of labour, women, progressive and peace movements throughout the world, as well as the movements and achievements of colonial peoples, black people, and other oppressed communities in seeking justice, human dignity and liberation.

Each year we produce two issues of our journal *Socialist History*, two historical pamphlets in our Occasional Papers series, and a members' newsletter.

We hold a lecture and debate in London every two months. In addition, we organise occasional conferences, book-launch meetings, and joint events with other sympathetic groups. We aim to hold more events outside London.

Join the Socialist History Society!

Members receive all our serial publications for the year at no extra cost and regular mailings about our activities. Individual members can vote at our January AGM and seek election to positions on the committee. Members are encouraged to participate in other ways.

Annual membership fees due January each year:

Individual waged	£18.00
Unwaged/student	£12.00
Abroad waged	£22.50
Abroad unwaged	£17.00
Institutions	£20.00
Institutions abroad	£25.00

To join, please send your name and address plus a cheque/PO payable to **Socialist History Society** to: The Secretary, SHS, 50 Elmfield Road, Balham, London SW17 8AL.